Dee b

Here b to picking up all
of your metters along the way...

Roadmap
to
RICHE$

Roadmap
to
RICHE$
7 Maps to Total Satisfaction

Tim Timmons
http//www.timtimmons.com

WINEPRESS WP PUBLISHING

ISBN 1-57921-158-5
Library of Congress Catalog Card Number: 98-75194

This book is dedicated to **Don and Dana Dixon** . . . faithful friends who have always been there to nudge me along—especially in the difficult times. . . . and to **Mack and Kay Strother** . . . without encouragement and support from the Dixon's and the Strother's, *Roadmap to <u>Riche$</u>* would be at the side of the road right now and 'Sir Richard Gladstone' would still be hanging out in a pet shop!

Acknowledgments

Jim Schmook . . . for his faithfulness as a production partner on this project.

Rob Wilson . . . for his faithfulness in pulling together the pieces.

Barbara Murphy . . . for her faithfulness in research and editing.

Mark and Kim Seigler . . . for their faithfulness in graphic creation and production.

Kay Matheson . . . for providing the most spectactular writing venue ever!

Contents

Introduction

On your way to financial wealth, pick up all of your other riches!

L ife's a bitch—and then you die!" What an outlook! If this is true, then it's all right to do whatever you please to get by or to get ahead . . . it's all right to view life with a cynic's eye . . . it's all right to leave relational wreckage in your path . . . it's all right to ignore other's needs and leave them in their own despair . . . it's all right to step on others in the process of your own survival in life's rat race. The reasoning goes, "As long as I can enjoy some degree of personal peace and prosperity for myself, nothing else and no one else matters."

LIFE WITHOUT HOPE

It's a moderate to strong case of narcissism that is becoming epidemic!

We are a world without a conscience! The results? Most who have caught this toxic attitude do not fully act it out, but we all are being affected by it daily! The attitude is so pervasive in our society that it saturates men and women at every level. You may not see it blatantly portrayed, but most every one of us feels it in moments of quiet desperation. You, personally, may easily find yourself experiencing one or more of the following . . .

- Your relationships aren't working!
- You find it difficult to trust anyone!
- You are overwhelmed with the information explosion to the point that you don't know how to think about most things . . . it's difficult to make decisions!
- You are dissatisfied with your work . . . it seems empty and meaningless!
- You experience great fears about your health . . . the confusion over the right diet (and you hate the taste) and the right exercise (and you're allergic to sweat)!
- You are filled with emotions and feelings, but are unable to express them appropriately or even express them at all!
- You are stressed out and don't even know how you feel!
- You feel that no one really understands you!
- You can't seem to accumulate enough security in your life . . . there never seems to be enough to make me feel secure!
- You experience a gnawing ache of loneliness, even when you're with people!
- You sense there may be a Higher Power out there, but He sure seems to be a Cosmic Killjoy with the major themes of negativism and condemnation! Who needs that?
- You're waiting and hoping for someone or something to bail you out of your life's trials!
- IT'S A LIFE WITH LITTLE OR NO HOPE!

TOXIC PEOPLE CREATE TOXIC MOVEMENTS

This toxic attitude can also be found within major movements. "We four and no more!" is the battle cry! No group seems to be exempt from this toxicity . . .

Sixties demonstrations . . . all that is big business and institutional is evil and must come down and we'll replace it with love—and chaos!

Liberals . . . people are unable to handle their own money and to govern their personal lives, therefore, we must tax them more and take care of them in their crippled state!

Conservatives . . . willing to take political losses, even reveling in them, for the sake of standing on 'their' righteous principles and the loss means that their voice doesn't even receive a thoughtful hearing!

Religious movements . . . spend most of their time together confessing the sins of the world, raising money with their 'ain't it awful and it's going to get worse unless you give to me' campaigns, and excusing themselves from the 'nasty now and now' by focusing totally on the 'sweet by and by.'

Racism and Rights activists . . . taking offense at every mention of their group in an unfavorable light—black, Hispanic, oriental, Jews, Arabs, gay, any religious flavor, abortion, anti-abortion, all manner of the disabled. There is no such thing as a good sense of humor with respect to these groupings any longer, because humor requires that you can laugh at yourself. By the way, being able to laugh at yourself is a sign of a healthy self-image. Go figure!

LIMITED AND FLAWED

But there is something very limiting and very flawed about this common world-view. The limiting factor is that life is limited to you—alone! To see life only from this viewpoint is to limit the possibilities of the vast wealth of learning from others, the loving support of others, and the substantial healing relationships can bring into your life. To live your life all alone, in a vacuum, is never to experience growth, love, or life itself! You have nothing greater than yourself in your life. You can never experience trust; there's no one there! Now that's depressing in itself! There is no reference point in your life other than you. You become your own god! But in this case, in the midst of your crises you have no one to turn to . . . you don't have a prayer!

Map Marker #7

Little boys believe in Santa Claus.
When they are a little older,
they don't believe in Santa Claus. Then, as adults,
they believe they are Santa Claus!
As children, people believe in God.
When they are a little older,
they don't believe in God. Then, as they grow up,
they believe that they are God!

This world-view is not only limiting but it is flawed! The flaw, simply put, is that this 'eat, drink, and be merry for tomorrow we die' approach doesn't produce much of the 'merry' in the process. On the contrary, the toxicity produces just the opposite. For instance, those who are screaming for their rights for the building of self-esteem, are damaging that self-esteem in the process. Those who attempt to help our families govern themselves are, in fact, crippling them further in the process.

More doesn't mean better. More seems to mean less! We have more recovery programs than ever before, but more people addicted than ever! It's an age of paradoxes. We have taller buildings, but shorter tempers; wider freeways, but narrower viewpoints; we spend more, but have less; we buy more, but enjoy it less.

We have bigger houses and smaller families; more conveniences, but less time; we have more degrees, but less sense; more knowledge, but less judgment; more experts, but more problems; more medicine, but less wellness.

We drink too much, smoke too much, spend too recklessly, laugh too little, drive too fast, get too angry too quickly, stay up too late, get up too tired, read too seldom, watch TV too much, and pray too seldom.

We have multiplied our possessions, but reduced our values. We talk too much, love too seldom and lie too often. We've learned how to make a living, but not a life; we've added years to life, not life to years.

We've been all the way to the moon and back, but have trouble crossing the street to meet the new neighbor.

We've conquered outer space, but not inner space; we've done larger things, but not better things; we've cleaned up the air, but polluted the soul;

We've split the atom, but not our prejudice; we write more, but learn less; plan more, but accomplish less.

We've learned to rush, but not to wait; we have higher incomes; but lower morals; more food but less appeasement; more acquaintances, but fewer friends; more effort but less success.

We build more computers to hold more information, to produce more copies than ever, but have less communication; we've become long on quantity, but short on quality.

These are the times of fast foods and slow digestion; tall men, and short character; steep profits, and shallow relationships.

These are the times of world peace, but domestic warfare; more leisure and less fun; more kinds of food, but less nutrition.

These are days of two incomes, but more divorce; of fancier houses, but broken homes. These are days of quick trips, disposable diapers, throwaway morality, one-night stands, overweight bodies, and pills that do everything from cheer, to calm, to kill. It's a time when there is much in the show window and nothing in the stockroom.

It's a time that is continually erupting and moving far too fast. It's like we're riding in the caboose on a runaway train with no one at the controls!

The primary flaw is that we do whatever more and enjoy it less! This personal dissatisfaction, sense of relational detachment and the feeling of quiet desperation have been launched and are being fueled by the toxic attitude that accompanies, "Life's a bitch, and then you die!" And, it's getting us nowhere—fast!

Map Marker #101

Even if you win the rat race, you're still a rat!

LIFE IS FULL OF PILES—AND HOPE!

"Life is difficult!" These words that open up Scott Peck's classic book, *The Road Less Traveled*, are a vital theme for us in order to make something positive out of our lives. This is contrary to the hopeless message of "Life's a bitch and then you die!" in that the message "Life is difficult!" gives a realistic viewpoint of life—difficult, but not hopeless!

Life is difficult. I visualize it as getting through the piles of life. There are two extremes. One extreme is where people try to live their lives on top of the pile—always positive. No matter what happens, they believe that they must be up. When you ask them how they are, it's always, "Great! Couldn't be better!" It doesn't matter the crisis, they are always saying, "Great!"

You look at this kind of person and you think, "I've never been up that high before! He must be snorting or smoking something."

The other extreme is where people live their lives underneath the pile—always negative. No matter what happens, they believe it won't work. They are continually saying, "I don't think it will work. I tried it before and it simply won't work!" They believe their entire life must be lived underneath the pile! They are as far down as the other extreme is up! Both are in the extreme. Life is not always on top of the pile . . . that's just not realistic and impossible to maintain! And, life is not always underneath the pile . . . it's just not that bad—always!

The reality is that LIFE IS FULL OF PILES! Your responsibility is to somehow get through those piles . . . you may go under it, over it, around it or shovel through it! This goes along with one of the most important MAP MARKERS . . .

Map Marker #5

It's not what happens to you, but how you handle what happens to you that matters most!

Life is a series of responsibilities lived out in the context of relationships. Handling what happens to you is responsibly dealing with those life circumstances that were either dealt to you as a matter of course, placed upon you by someone else or self-inflicted. Handling your life responsibly is life management. A good friend of mine who logs several hours per week on the golf courses of this world said, "Life management is like golf. To be successful in golf is to manage the course well. So, life management is course management!" Wherever that little ball lands from a slice or a hook, you find it and maneuver it toward the next flag. (I say flag, because I see more of the flag waving than I do the actual hole, when I play golf.)

I have noticed that most people suffer from having to do with the unknown more than the known. Years ago I picked up a T-shirt on Maui that says it best,

---

Map Marker #149

"We know that for every door that closes
another one always opens,
but those hallways are terrifying!"

Roadmap to **RICHE$** is meant to be a true roadmap for your life—instruction in life management. In addition to the book, use the workbook and audio tapes to customize your personal roadmap to *RICHE$*. Also, keep up with the latest materials, products, tests, tours, seminars and workshops to empower you toward a richer life through our website .

There are only two primary rules of the road:

Rule #1- GAINING- You're responsible for picking up your own riches!

Rule #2- GIVING- You are responsible for giving them back!

The following story puts the intent of this book into focus:

Brooks was very careful to do everything right in his life. When he died and was ushered into Heaven, he faced the welcome sight of an imposing character that identified himself as Peter. After a few simple questions, Peter invited Brooks to follow him on a quick tour before entering into Heaven proper.

Peter led Brooks down a long, beautiful street that was lined with what seemed like millions of warehouses. Each warehouse had a name over the front door. This particular warehouse had Brooks Jamison in huge script over the entrance. Peter motioned for Brooks to enter. When Brooks walked through the doorway, he was overwhelmed with all kinds of packages stacked to the ceiling and the warehouse went as far as he could see. As he examined the packages, he discovered that each one had a tag on it with his name written on it. Brooks asked Peter what these packages were all about . . .

And Peter said, "These are the blessings and riches that were earmarked for you while on planet earth, but you didn't pick them up!"

Each of us has a warehouse full of riches waiting to be delivered. All that is necessary for you to receive them is to identify them and prepare yourself to use them wisely. Perfection is not necessary. That's impossible! You don't have to be perfect, but you are required to take what you have and who you are and make something good out of it! Remember this map marker . . .

Map Marker #4

A flawed diamond is better than a perfect brick!

May this book empower you to pick up all of the riches you want, so that you become truly wealthy!

Chapter 1

What's Holding You Back?

In 1975 I moved my family from Highland Park in Dallas, Texas, to Newport Beach, California. Highland Park and Newport Beach are two of the most beautiful, high-rent districts in our world! In Texas I logged many hours working with some of the wealthiest people from a long line of old wealth. In addition to all of the wealth in Newport Beach, there is the gorgeous coastline, the classy restaurants, the parade of luxury sports cars and sedans, the large, sprawling mansions on the islands and in the hillsides, and the nearly perfect weather! Newport Beach is one of seven places in all of the world where the ocean air and the desert air meet (the Greek Islands is another).

Just as I had found in Texas, Newport Beach was a wonderful paradise with great poverty on every hand. Over the next 23 years I have spent thousands of hours counseling the wealthy and the poor in southern California.

EXTREMELY WEALTHY, BUT POOR

One of my first speaking experiences in Newport Beach was one of the most memorable of my life. I was invited to join 14 or 15 multi-millionaires for lunch at a local hotel suite. I was seated at the table and told that I wouldn't be speaking until they introduced themselves to me. That was fine, but little did I know what was about to happen . . .

The first man told a brief story of his life. He rehearsed his background, listed his houses around the world, his 3 yachts, and his annual income of $9 million from 3 patents he owned. This was quite a story and I was really getting into it, thinking that it was very good that I was invited to 'hang out' with these guys. Then his entire mood shifted to an intense sadness. He began to tear up as he told of his personal and family losses. His tears turned into sobs. Although his final statement was muffled from his sobbing, it was the clearest I had ever heard from a grown man. He said, "I have everything and yet I've lost everything that is most important to me!" What a dramatic turn of emotion and mood!

In the midst of his sobbing he nudged the man next to him and the second man went through the same exercise. I was impressed how his story of financial success seemed to lift the mood of the room. Yachts . . . 34 classic cars . . . a home in Europe . . . in Mexico . . . and in San Francisco . . . The sadness from the first man was almost forgotten, until this second man went down the very same path. He broke into tears as he shifted gears. He finally regained enough composure that he was able to get it out that he, too, had lost two wives and lives without any contact with his children. It was a pitiful sight!

This went on throughout the rest of the men around the table, until it was my turn. The chairman of the day then said, "Can you share any insights at all that might help each of us to recapture the true riches of life?" What a question! What an introduction!

I shared the first thoughts that came into my head, "When I walked into this room, I felt that I was certainly the poorest man in the room. But now I am convinced that I am the wealthiest!"

You see, on your way to financial riches, the tendency is not to pick up all of the other riches available to you. So, when you reach your financial pinnacle, it feels so empty—so dissatisfying!

I have often thought about that meeting and have developed that thinking into this book. For some reason, there are masses of people who seemingly 'have it all', but are very poor in their soul! Whatever they are doing, apparently, it is not the most effective thing to do to produce the true riches of life—true wealth!

Map Marker #27

If you keep doing what you're doing,
you'll keep getting what you're getting!

The true riches are available to everyone, but they are easily missed or devoured. True wealth is more than money. It's the balancing of several riches. In addition to the financial, true wealth must include your relationships, peace of mind, job satisfaction, your health, feeling good, and a spiritual base. The challenge is to pick up all of them that are meant for you!

7 LIFE PARASITES

It's one thing to accumulate your riches, but quite another to hang on to them. In order for you to pick up all of your riches, you must first get a handle on the things that hold you back from picking them up and possessing them for your enjoyment. In the process of counseling several thousand people from all walks of life and in consulting hundreds of corporate executives and owners, I have discovered 7 life parasites that suck the life out of you. These parasites will keep you from picking up your riches, hanging on to your riches, and enjoying them! Let's briefly look at each one . . .

UNSAFE

Possibly the most common and most destructive of the parasites is what I call **UNSAFE**—insecure, the ache of loneliness, the feeling of insignificance, an emptiness that gnaws away at the inner soul. You desperately need a shelter—a place where you are affirmed, a home, a warm relational base which empowers you—a safe place. You'll do most anything to get it!

If you play a role that you think others might like and find out that they do, you are really in a predicament. Now, you are liked, but not actually you, but the role that you've been playing. It's possible to play this role for quite some time, but sooner or later your role will burn itself out. I think this has a lot to do with what is known as the 'mid-life crisis' that so many experience. The role is played for quite some time, until you experience a 'wake-up call.' You wake up to the fact that this isn't what you want. Even though you have been playing this role out for several years, this wake-up is a refreshing shock to your system—and to those around you! For years I've encouraged people to "have your mid-crises early and often!" The sooner you rid yourself of your pseudo-roles and become brutally honest with who you are and what you want, the quicker you will make the rest of your life the best of your life!

We are the masters of the surfacey relationship, but the surfacey isn't very satisfying. "How are you? . . . Fine! . . . Job going well? . . . How about the kids? . . . Well, except for the one terrorist, we're doing very well! . . . Hey, good talking with you!" That could easily have been a conversation with one of your 'best' friends!

Think of the numbers of people you come in contact with each day. It's impossible to go into any kind of 'in depth' relationship with many of them or any of them at all! Like balls on a pool table that randomly bump into one another, you make your way to the next appointment, the next meeting, the next errand, the next carpool destination, but you rarely connect with anyone in a meaningful encounter—at least, not enough! Added to this lack of meaningful connection with other people is the jungle-like atmosphere in the corporate marketplace, the stressful struggles within your own family, and the painful betrayal and disappointment you experience in those 'friendships' in which you placed your trust.

Maybe the biggest offense of this particular parasite is found in what is supposed to be the safest place of all—the home. Yet the vast majority of people in our world grow up in what has come to be known as a dysfunctional home. I am convinced that every home is dysfunctional to some degree, since humans live there.

Functional or dysfunctional, the home ought to be the ultimate shelter, but it seldom is. Years ago, the University of Rhode Island produced a study stating that the most dangerous place to be, outside of war, was the American home. Everyday produces more information about how prevalent the world of abuse has become. Most abuse happens in the home by family members and friends!

Possibly the saddest situation of all is when a couple or family has a beautiful house, but are unable to make it into a home—no matter how rich they may be in other areas of life. The ache of loneliness may be the worst pain you can experience. We call it by many other names—anger, depression, burned out, disappointment, sadness, etc., but the core of these painful feelings is a sense of being all alone with no one there to connect with your inner soul.

BOTTOMLINE PARASITIC PROBLEM? The core of this parasitic problem is the tendency to look for the wrong things in relationships. The tendency is to look for acceptance and approval from others. You can't allow yourself to get into this mode or you'll certainly be disappointed—even devastated!

When you look for personal approval from your relationships, you give too much power to other people. If you empower someone to give you your needed approval, you are also giving them the power to disapprove and discount you. If you place others in this position of power in your life, you will become extremely needy—almost addicted to certain relationships. You will fixate on a person as the answer to your desperate needs! Now, you must do anything that is necessary to keep this new 'drug of choice' in your life—smother, control, manipulate, cling to them! These actions fill the prescription precisely for failure in your relationships! The life that you want will be sucked out of you and the relationship!

UNWISE

Most know what's right and what's wrong. The question, "What is the right thing to do?" will be answered clearly in most situations. However, the real tough issues in life have to do with what's wise and what's foolish. What is the wise thing to do? **UNWISE** is one of the most pervasive of the parasites in that it affects everything you think or do!

Wisdom is one of the most valuable qualities to acquire in your life. Solomon, known as the wisest man who ever lived, believed wisdom to embody the greatest of life's benefits. He said, "Long life is in her (wisdom's) right hand; in her (wisdom's) left hand are riches and honor."

Wisdom is the acquisition of a full perspective on life—balanced and clear. To be unwise is to have a faulty perspective on life—imbalanced and fuzzy. There are as many faulty perspectives as there are people and situations, but here are the three most common:

#1-PARTIAL PERSPECTIVE. Partial perspective is not having enough knowledge to decide or act wisely. When I talk with a frantic wife who is talking about her jerky husband, I tend to agree with her side. Then, when I meet her husband, I want to give him a medal for living with her! That's a partial perspective that will always give an imbalanced and fuzzy picture.

#2-PREJUDICED PERSPECTIVE. Whereas a partial perspective is when you don't have all of the facts, the prejudiced perspective is when you don't want the facts. The facts might mess up what you already believe!

A man sat in front of his doctor, claiming that he knew that he was dead. The doctor assured him that he wasn't dead—depressed, maybe, but very much alive. Nothing would change the patient's mind on the issue. So, the doctor sent him on a research project to the medical library. The research would conclusively prove that "dead men don't bleed."

When the patient finished his research, he returned to see his doctor. The doctor asked, "What did the research say?" "Well," said the patient, "it is clear that the medical literature says it clearly that dead men don't bleed." "Perfect!" replied the doctor. The doctor immediately went over to the patient, stuck a needle in his arm, and the man began to bleed. Without any hesitation the patient jumped up and proclaimed, "Dead men **do** bleed!" Now, that's a prejudiced perspective! Don't confuse me with the facts. My mind is already made up!

#3-PASSIVE PERSPECTIVE. A passive perspective is when you have the facts, but don't act upon them. You are committed, but not involved in the behavior that the commitment requires. This is, by far, an epidemic in our society! Committed, but not involved! You know what to do in your marriage, but don't do it. You know what to do with your children, but don't do it. You know what to do in the midst of a conflict, but don't do it. You know what to do with your priorities, but you don't do it. It's like the kamikaze pilot who made 33 missions. He was committed, but not involved!

Map Marker #184

"You need good judgment."
"Where do you get good judgment?"
"Experience!"
"And where do you get experience?"
"Bad judgment!"

When you're unwise, you are into defective thinking. This defective thinking will suck the life out of your journey toward picking up and possessing your life's riches!

UNFULFILLED

The 3rd life parasite that can hold you back from picking up and possessing all of your riches in life is **UNFULFILLED**. No matter how much money or power that you are able to amass in your life endeavors, you still may not feel fulfilled in your work. There is something about job satisfaction that is very important to your overall sense of wealth. It's more than a cash-flow problem. When you feel that your work is a bummer, that you dread to go there, that what you are doing is not meaningful, that you don't fit or that you have no work, there is a gut-level dissatisfaction that is demoralizing to everything else you want to do. Your work is good for you and is a vital expression of who you are.

The competition and, sometimes, cut-throat nature of the work-place sets you up for a defensive stance with people. Whenever anything goes wrong, the knee-jerk reaction by most is to find someone to blame. Most become teflon-like targets and are looking for a velcro-like person to stick the blame on. If you don't stay alert to what's happening, you can find yourself the target of someone's blame for the latest crisis or blunder.

One friend of mine said that he had been climbing the corporate ladder for 34 years only to realize that his ladder was leaning up against the wrong building.

More and more people, thinking they have some degree of security in their profession, are being jarred into a grim reality that they will not receive their retirement, are not appreciated as much as they had thought, and won't even have enough money to buy their own gold watch at the end of their work career. The truth is that there is no way for you to find total security with respect to your job. The real insecurity is to be found, not in the job, itself, but in the sense of fulfillment that you feel in doing your job. Lack of fulfillment is another vicious parasite that will suck the life out of your riches!

UNHEALTHY

The 4th life parasite is **UNHEALTHY**. A few years ago I was consoling a young lady who was distraught over the suffering that her grandfather was experiencing. When I went to see him, I encountered a man who told me his story that was filled with regret. He told me of his family that he loved so much, his home that he missed, and his work that he had built to an impressive entity. He knew that he had been greatly blessed with family, friends, home, and work, but he could not enjoy any of these blessings. You see, he was dying a slow death due to emphysema. He had smoked 2-3 packs of cigarettes per day for over 35 years. Now, at 56, after years of suffering, he was unable to breathe and was told by his doctor that he would surely die within the next few weeks. He said something that so many have said to me over the years. "I'd give anything I have to be able to live just a little longer!"

You can build your wealth to whatever level you can dream, but without your health you will not enjoy it! The loss of your health, for whatever reason, cannot be regained through a talented doctor, an efficient and caring hospital, or through any amount of money! This parasite is more terminal than any of the others, because this one not only sucks the enjoyment out of your riches, but could take your life!

UNPRODUCTIVE

The most insidious and the possibly the most invisible of the life parasites is the 5th. I call it **UNPRODUCTIVE**. Productivity is a human necessity to be truly rich. In 1990 I resigned from being the head of a large, non-profit organization that had a long, track record of helping people and their families. I had approximately 70 staff working for me. No matter what I chose to do on a given day, I knew that this people-helper organization was doing many good things and was truly productive in every way. I had a real sense of satisfaction and knew the good feelings for productivity, because of my leadership in founding this effective entity. The week that I resigned I found myself in a very different situation. If I was going to do anything productive today, then I had to do it myself.

There are lots of measuring sticks for productivity. There are two primary measurements—short-term and long-term. When I get that first look and feel of a book that I have written , I feel a sense of real productivity. When I am called in to help a person in distress and feel that I have been successful in easing that distress, then I feel a sense of productivity. When I am handed the check for speaking to a corporate audience, I feel a sense of productivity. When I have enough money in my pocket to pay cash for something, I feel a sense of productivity. Now, these are illustrations of a short-term measuring stick on productivity.

Short-term productivity has more instant results and has to do with receiving and spending what you have. Long-term productivity has to do with how well you invest your time, talent, and treasure.

Although productivity has to do with your time, your talent, and your treasure, it's your money, or lack of it, that seems to get into the way of enjoying all of your riches. Money becomes either your goal or a vehicle to reach your life goals. It isn't money that is the root of all evil, but the love of money—the focus on it to the exclusion of people and principles.

Money! You go to school to learn to earn it. We spend 40 to 60 hours a week earning it, have countless thoughts and plans on how to handle it, hours in the shopping malls spending it, worry that we won't have enough of it, dream and scheme to find ways to acquire more of it, argue over it, despair over losing it, which leads to suicide and all kinds of sicknesses, . . . greed has let to crime, absence of it leads to despair and depression. Money can be a real problem!

Wasting or worshipping money is a minor problem compared to what we do with the greatest commodity we own—TIME! Time is your most important bank account!

Imagine there is a bank that credits your account each morning with $86,400. It carries over no balance from day to day. Every evening deletes whatever part of the balance you failed to use during the day. What would you do? Draw out every cent, of course! Each of us has such a bank. Its name is TIME. Every morning, it credits you with 86,400 seconds. Every night it writes off, as lost, whatever of this you have failed to invest to good purpose. It carries over no balance. It allows no overdraft. Each day it opens a new account for you. Each night it burns the remains of the day. If you fail to use the day's deposits, the loss is yours. There is no going back. There is no drawing against the "tomorrow." You must live in the present on today's deposits. Invest it so as to get from it the utmost in health, happiness and success!

The clock is running. You must make the most of today. To realize the value of ONE YEAR, ask a student who failed a grade. To realize the value of ONE MONTH, ask a mother who gave birth to a premature baby. To realize the value of ONE WEEK, ask the editor of a weekly newspaper. To realize the value of ONE DAY, ask a daily wage laborer with kids to feed. To realize the value of ONE HOUR, ask the lovers who are waiting to meet. To realize the value of ONE MINUTE, ask a person who missed the train. To realize the value of ONE SECOND, ask a person who just avoided an accident. To realize the value of ONE MILLISECOND, ask the person who won a silver medal in the Olympics.

Remember that time waits for no one. Yesterday is history. Tomorrow is a mystery. Today is a gift. That's why it's called the present!

The productivity parasite is a waster of time, talent, and treasure! It's always at work to suck the life and enjoyment out of your riches!

UNHAPPY

The 6th life parasite is called **UNHAPPY**. Unhappy is tied to your emotions and feelings. If you are in turmoil on the inside, you can't enjoy your accumulated riches.

In my experience, unhappy people have one thing in common with one another. Unhappy people are looking for happiness in the wrong places. The normal places to look for happiness are people, places and things. The tendency is to look outside yourself, but it won't work! People can only contribute to your happiness; they can't make your happiness. Places can't make you happy, either. I've traveled throughout the world and those places can contribute to your happiness. And, things can't make you happy. Things are fun, but they can't make you happy! If you count on people, places, and things to make you happy, then you will know unhappiness soon!

Another thing about happiness is that by its very definition, it is temporary and fleeting. Happiness comes from the word happenings.

Happenings are based upon your circumstances of the day and those circumstances change as often as the wind. There is a better way to reach happiness more often than not and that is joy. Joy is an underlying feeling that keeps the big picture on the circumstances. Joy recognizes that your circumstances go up and down. Therefore, you may be happy one minute and the next unhappy. Joy, however, is an ongoing experience that rests on a more complete perspective on life. Joy is the ability to enjoy the scenery while on a detour! (We'll discuss how to turn unhappy into happy later on in the book.)

It's easy to see that if you focus on happiness as a primary goal in life, you are likely to experience lots of unhappiness along the way. This unhappy state can be very discouraging and suck the life out of enjoying your riches.

UNPLUGGED

As you can readily see the life parasites serve to distract you away from what's most important. This brings us to a critical map marker . . .

Map Marker #103

When you find yourself up to your waist in alligators, it's easy to forget that your original intent was to drain the swamp!

The 7th life parasite is the ultimate result of the other 6. I call it being **UNPLUGGED**. One of the most simple, yet profound life principles I've ever encountered is . . .

Map Marker #13

Everything works best when it's plugged in!

Being unplugged is when you are out of control—no purpose or direction to your life! It reminds me of what the Captain of an airline announced to his passengers on a bizarre flight: "Ladies and gentlemen: This is your Captain speaking. We're traveling West across the Pacific Ocean. In a few hours you will be able to look down and see land. When that happens, we're going to start looking for a big city with an airport. If we find one before our fuel runs out, we'll land. Then we'll figure out where we are and decide where we want to go next. In the meantime, folks, just sit back and relax and enjoy your trip!

UNPLUGGED FROM WHAT?

There is a lesson to be learned in the midst of pain, suffering, and crisis that seems to slip through the cracks, when things are going well. From the vantage point of the counseling room, the hospital room, ICU, the loss of something or someone precious or in the moments of quiet desperation, there is a cry for help to what many call a Higher Power. This cry comes from atheists and agnostics, as well as those who fashion themselves as 'true believers.' No matter the religious or non-religious background, the cry erupts out of utter hopelessness.

This same cry is in evidence of what has been defined as a hole in the soul. It's a hunger and thirst for a satisfying of the spiritual dimension of your inner-most being—your soul! All studies demonstrate a renewed search and rush into that which is spiritual. This is evidenced by such things as the massive interest in the psychic hotlines, the craze for talking to your loved ones on 'the other side', and some of the major themes of the New Age movement. There is a fascination with all sorts of objects and techniques used to seek advice and strength from the spirit world.

You need a reference point to make sense out of your life—a basis for moral thinking and values. For this to be an adequate reference point, it must be greater than you and what you have created. The great philosophers of the past called this inner longing and need for an adequate reference point—God. I think of it as a God-shaped, spiritual vacuum that can only be filled by being plugged into a real God-consciousness.

You can attempt to fill up that hole in your soul with everything else—alcohol, chemicals, work, relationships, religion, money, or things, but nothing else will satisfy. I see it as a need to be reconnected with your Creator. Many people come to this understanding through the process of elimination—nothing else works! Why is it that more and more, you hear the same story or reason for success from the world-class athletes, highly-honored actors, survivors of deadly diseases or tragedies, and those who have struggled with addictions? Not only is it increasing, but it has become more acceptable!

Even the scientific community is rallying around the evidence for an intelligent Creator or Designer! Listen to the world of astral physics:

- Astral physicist, Bernard Carr says, "One would have to conclude either that the features of the universe invoked in support of the Anthropic Principle (that the universe is keenly balanced for human life to exist on earth) are only coincidences or that the universe was indeed tailor-made for life. I will leave it to the theologians to ascertain the identity of the tailor."

- Vera Kistiakowsky (MIT physicist/past President of the Association of Women in Science) says, "The exquisite order displayed by our scientific understanding of the physical world calls for the divine."
- Arno Penzias- (Nobel prize winner) says, "Astronomy leads us to a unique event, a universe which was created out of nothing, one with the very delicate balance needed to provide exactly the conditions required to permit life, and one which has an underlying (one might say 'supernatural') plan."
- Allan Sandage- (winner of the Crafoord prize in Astronomy) says, "I find it quite improbable that such order came out of chaos. There has to be some organizing principle. God to me is a mystery, but is the explanation for the miracle of existence, why there is something instead of nothing."
- Robert Griffiths- (Heinemann Prize in Mathematical Physics) adds, "If we need an atheist for a debate, I have to go to the philosophy department. The physics department isn't much use anymore."

Mankind becomes unplugged from its Creator and feels the need to plug back in! There is a tale of God calling His human children to form a great circle for a game. In that circle we ought all to be standing, linked together with lovingly joined hands, facing towards the Light in the center, which is God . . . . seeing our fellow creatures all around the circle in the light of that central love, which shines on them and beautifies their faces . . . . But instead, we have each one, turned our backs upon God and the circle of our fellows, and faced the other way, so that we can see neither the Light at the center nor the faces in the circle. And it is difficult even to join hands with our fellows! Therefore, instead of playing God's game, we play, each one, our own selfish little game . . .

Each one of us wishes to be the center, and there is blind confusion and no true knowledge of God, our selves, or others . . .
This is what is meant by being unplugged!

UNPACK YOUR BAGS

The parasites suck the life out of you and force you into some kind of coping strategy to get by and to get through your stresses and difficulties you face. You learn how to cope both by trial and error and, many times, you are taught these strategies by your parents and other mentors. These coping mechanisms are packed away in your psyche for use whenever necessary. This is the baggage you carry with you throughout your life.

You may not have packed all of your own bags yourself, but you choose to take them with you. In this book, you will learn that it's time to unpack your bags.

PARASITIC WRECKAGE

The 7 life parasites wreak havoc upon your life at whatever level they attach themselves to you. Even one or two can be devastating! Whether or not you allow them to suck your life away from your riches, you can easily be distracted by them away from enjoying the riches you have accumulated. The wreckage of these parasites causes you to be vulnerable and fragile. Rather than empower and enrich you, they disempower and drain you!

Here is a partial listing of the parasitic wreckage:

- Pushed to be a reactionary rather than pro-active!
- Pushed to repeat bad or unwise choices—a predictable cycle!
- Pushed into perpetual dissatisfaction with your life, loved ones, and livelihood!
- Pushed into feelings of worthlessness!
- Pushed into running with the crowd!

- Pushed into an over-commitment to busyness!
- Pushed to blame everything and everybody for your unfavorable circumstances!
- Pushed into paralysis—stuck in the quagmire of a problem!
- Pushed into medicating the pain to avoid facing your problems!

Possibly the most devastating factor that lies behind these life parasites is the lure and promise of something wonderful while delivering just the opposite! No one seeks to take parasites into his body. But you may be lured into something that sounds good with a parasite attached. This is the same as rat poison. The rat poison mixture is 96% nutritional and only 4% poison! This is exactly how the life parasites are taken in!

In other words, it's a trap! When it comes to riches, the traps are set everywhere. One of the basic traps is what I call the IT TRAP! If I could drive that kind of car, that would be it. If I could make that much money, that would be it. If I could live up there in that house, that would be it. If I could get married, that would be it. If we could have children, that would be it. If I had that position of power, that would be it. Then, when you get to IT, you find that somebody took IT! IT isn't there! That's the trap the parasites set for you . . .

Getting a handle on the life parasites gives you a better understanding of what keeps holding you back from picking up and possessing all of your riches . . .

Map Marker #11

It doesn't matter whether you win or you lose . . .
until you lose!

Chapter 2

Minding Your Own *RICHE$!*

Map Marker #73

He who believes he can and he who believes
he can't are both right!

The power of your mind is phenomenal! It is true that "whatever your mind can conceive and believe, you can achieve!" Whatever you set out to do in your life, you must set your mind to it!

Map Marker #25

You can commit yourself to something
over and over again,
but if you don't talk your mind into
going along with it,
your commitment will fizzle out!

Illustrations of the limiting power are plenty. You can take a clear glass cylinder and place it in your aquarium with the fish inside. The fish will continually bump into the glass walls, day after day. Then, after a couple of weeks, remove the cylinder and the fish will remain inside the space of the cylinder as if it is still there. Or, tie up a mighty elephant with a rope and a stake. He will attempt to pull away for a few days. Now, remove the stake and he will not move away from this area. People experience the same thing.

We have all kinds of cylinders and stakes placed upon us so that we don't break free of these entanglements. This power of the mind is not only true in a limiting sense, but in a freeing sense as well. If the Wright Brothers had listened to their critics, you might be driving long distances and never flying. If runners believed that the 4 minute mile was impossible, then it would never have been broken.

Now, keep in mind that you can't believe for someone else. You must believe in your own mind! When it comes to your riches, I have come to realize that you can have anything you want, but not everything! You just don't have that much time! If you are going to pick up and possess the riches you want, *you must do it yourself!*

Map Marker #83

Remember the man who sent a rose to his sweetheart every day for 45 days . . . she married the delivery boy!

MINDING Your Own Riches

OPERATING POWER OF MINDING

Your mind is the control-center of everything that's you! It's "the brains of your outfit!"

In addition to being a control-center, your mind is also a giant tape recorder. It has efficiently recorded everything you've ever said, heard, seen, felt, and done! Through hypnotism you can be taken back through your life all the way to childhood. If you're asked to write your name the way you did at 16, you'll write it just the way your mind recorded it when you were 16. When you're asked to write your name the way you did at 7, you will carefully print it out exactly the you did at 7. The operating power of the mind is incredible!

The mind has also been compared to a computer! What you put into a computer is what comes out and the same is true for your mind. If you store negative information in your mind, negatives must come out! Garbage in—garbage out! It's like the "sowing and reaping" principle. Once the seed thought (positive or negative) has been sown, the feelings and actions which are reaped from it will be the same as the seed.

The operating power of the mind can also affect physical ailments. There's an increasing amount of evidence being gathered to support the notion that people even choose things like tumors, influenza, arthritis, heart disease, "accidents" and many other infirmities—including cancer—which have always been considered things that just happen to people. In treating the "terminally ill" patients, some researchers now believe that helping the patient not to want the disease, in any form, may be a means of turning the internal killer around. Some cultures treat pain in this way, taking complete power over the mind and making self-control synonymous with the control of the mind.

The mind, which is composed of 10 billion, billion working parts, has enough storage capacity to accept 10 new facts every second. It has been conservatively estimated that the human mind can store an amount of information equivalent to one hundred trillion words, and that all of us use but a tiny fraction of this storage space. What you carry around wth you in your head is a powerful instrument!

If you are going to take control of your life, you must take control of your mind—the control-center! And it's up to you to take control of your own mind, then you can start being, feeling, and behaving in the ways you choose!

Map Marker #170

As you think, you are.
As you think, you feel.
As you think, you behave.

OVERALL PROSPERITY OF 'MINDING'

If you want to 'mind your own riches', you must control your own mind. And, if you want to control your mind, then you must feed it selectively! Minding is a form of mediation.

Meditation is the selective feeding of the mind. The most popular form of meditation is an 'emptying' process, but true meditation doesn't occur in a vacuum. True meditation involves feeding your mind!

I must confess that meditation is the most difficult activity I have ever attempted, yet I know of no other activity that is more life-changing! The results of meditation are endless! More valuable than anything else is that meditation will widen your perspective on your self, your relationships and your future! When you can 'mind' your own riches, you'll be able to make decisions about what you really want in life.

Several years ago, I became hooked on the process of meditation. I heard a man speak on the subject and decided to try it. His bent on meditation was that it could be a change-agent in your life. There was one particular area of my personality that I really wanted to change, and that was my nasty habit of going berserk when anyone messed with my car! I knew the habit had to go or I'd soon be traveling the road alone for lack of friends.

Since over the years I have chosen the Bible as a major source of insight and wisdom, I began meditating on a paragraph that seemed to reflect some of the change I wanted. The beginning of the paragraph was, "Consider it all joy when you encounter various trials; knowing that the testing of your faith produces endurance . . . ." Little did I know how much this tiny principle would begin a change in me.

As I moved into the process of overhauling my mind by meditating on this paragraph, some exciting things happened. I experienced an all-out war on my nice, new car! It seemed like every parking lot had a roving destroyer just waiting for me to leave my car so he could dent or scratch it! And around every corner was a car sledgehammer with my car's license number on it! Within three weeks after I started meditating, I experienced four major accidents! My car was demolished! I found myself suffering from automobile paranoia.

But in each of these "various trials" (from scratches to scrapes to smashes) something strange was happening to my normal reaction-style. At each occurrence, just when I was ready to move into 'berserkness,' a sign lit up in my mind's eye. It said, "consider it all joy . . . when you encounter various trials; knowing that the testing of your faith produces endurance!" When this appeared, I was reminded of the bigger picture (a much wider perspective on life) and chose not to blow up. Needless to say, I was impressed with my new behavior pattern, because I was in control! By expanding your perspective on life, meditation gives your 'control-center' more options to choose from when it's time for action. I prescribe meditation for those seeking counsel more than anything else! It shouldn't necessarily be used as the total cure for a problem, but it does play an important, supporting role. As a psychological tranquilizer the effect of meditation calms you down an lets you think about your situation—which is expanding your perspective on your life!

This kind of meditation brings into focus the most genuine prosperity you could ever possess—your riches! Peace of mind, wisdom, control of annoying problems, a greater sensitivity during 'various trials,' hope for personal change and growth, and so on. Whatever your stress problem, you'll find meditation can be a mental adrenaline that will boost you into the 'controls' of you and your riches!

OVERHAULING PROCESS OF MEDITATION

The overhauling process is preparatory work for 'psychological digestion.' The mental food you order for meditation will determine the kinds of digestion you'll experience. If you order junk food for your mind, you may experience problems in your psychological digestion—like psychological heartburn!

Although I have found the Bible to be the most satisfying source for my menu, there are great works of literature that you may find helpful to you. When I spend time in the Wisdom literature of the Bible, I find all kinds of nuggets from the Psalms and Proverbs. These are especially applicable for a daily diet of meditation.

After ordering your mental food, you must bite into it. A paragraph contains a basic unit of thought and seems to work best for a bite-sized chunk in the overhauling process. Next, you must chew it. The chewing process is extremely important, as the more you think about your mental food the deeper it sinks into your psyche. Chew on a paragraph or a principle for about a week. Write it out on a 3 by 5 card. You can put it on your desk, fasten it to your refrigerator, clip it on your visor in the car, or carry it with you so you can keep chewing on it throughout the week. Finally, you must swallow your mental food. Swallowing is the process of applying the principles of life to your life-situations, making wise choices which are in line with the principles.

No matter how you meditate, make the choice to do it!

<hr>

Map Marker #77

The mind is not a thing to be filled up,
but a fire to be kindled!

<hr>

Minding YOUR OWN Riches

THE WORLD ACCORDING TO **YOU**!

I'll never forget one of the most powerful experiences of my life in front of the TV set. My very young daughters and I were watching this new show called "Mr. Rogers Neighborhood" and he was just a little much for me at the time, until I saw my girls' faces. He was focusing in on each person's nose. He made a major point out of the fact that no two people had the same nose. Your nose is so unique and totally and completely yours. My girls were mesmerized with Mr. Rogers and with their noses. It was powerful! Although we moved passed the nose as a mark of uniqueness, this uniqueness principle has always been a theme at our house.

You are an unrepeatable miracle of the Creator—a one-of-a-kind masterpiece! There is no other person exactly like you! Your finger-print is your physical identification card—totally unique! Your finger-print sets you apart from all others and marks you as totally and completely unique.

As technology has increased, and thanks to the O.J. Simpson trial, you repeatedly hear about your DNA. DNA is another identification of your uniqueness. It is your internal identification card—your own genetic code! No one else has your personal code!

Understanding this sort of uniqueness lays the foundation of one of the most vital principles of life. Not only are you created as an unrepeatable miracle—a unique masterpiece; *your choices, your preferences, your performance and your wants are also unique to you!*

This presents several truths that you must factor into your lifestyle.

First, *comparison to others is a foolish exercise!* Although there are some comparisons that are helpful, too much comparison has become debilitating. Your primary competition is with yourself and how much you are improving in whatever endeavor. Therefore, comparison is really useless! How are you doing? How are you progressing? If you pay attention to you and your progress, then competition in the marketplace will take care of itself!

Second, *consulting experts has a limited benefit!* You are the expert on you! No one else knows you as you do. So many people seek out and pay dearly to counselors, gurus, spiritual leaders, or other experts to find their purpose in life or to motivate them toward their mission in life. Ultimately, this is a waste of time and money, unless the 'expert' that you consult pulls your purpose and motivation out of you! As we'll see later in this book, your purpose is inside you and no one can tell you what it is.

This principle also applies to your business. You may consult others to see how they have handled similar problems or situations, but you're the expert on how to run your business. You know your team, your colleagues, your boss, and your situation better than anyone else.

By the way, this same principle is especially true when it comes to parenting your children. You are the one who knows your child best. That's your job, should you accept it, as a parent! I have never answered a question in my parenting seminar/workshops with re-spect to how to handle a situation. I always threw the question out to the audience of parents and asked them to share what they had done in 'similar' situations. What a powerful dynamic throughout the audience! I, the 'expert' was in town. They had paid money to hear me speak on parenting. But they went away feeling that, for the most part, they knew what to do with their kids. All you need to know are basic principles of parenting. You already know your child—the best!

So listen and learn from the 'experts', but take it all with a grain of salt and adapt what you hear to your particular scene. Glean the life principles from the 'experts,' so that you can make wise deci-sions on your own! Seek out the 'experts' who will empower you, not make you dependent upon them for power—that's disempowering!

Third, *contrasts are more the norm than comparisons*! Since you are uniquely different from every other person on the planet, then em-phasize this difference in your thinking. If you see others as different from you, you are less likely to try to change them to be more like you. If you see yourself as different from others, you tend to make individual decisions about your own life, rather than go along with the decisions of the crowd. If you see yourself as different from oth-ers, you are more likely to see how you fit and how others fit—whether on a team, in a friendship, in a marriage or in a business partnership.

Your junk is someone else's treasure!

What makes you sick can be another's delight!

One man smokes for 93 years and dies of old age while another man never smokes and dies of lung cancer at age 52. One person can eat piles of food and never gain a pound while another must limit his intake and still gains weight.

What's good for you is not necessarily good for someone else!

For you to mind your own riches, you must learn to celebrate your differences! And, the celebration of differences is the foundation step for building a solid unity!

A BILLION SPERM

When your father deposited sperm into your mother to get your mother's egg, there were over a billion sperm released. Think of it! It was like a swimming race with over a billion contestants and YOU WON! You beat out over a billion others to become YOU! That's how unique you are! If you really contemplate this for over 30 seconds, you will want to strut more confidently the rest of the day!

APPOINT YOURSELF AS CEO OF YOUR LIFE!

I view my life as a corporation. It's Tim Timmons, Inc. With this in mind I view my life plan as my personal business plan. This includes my vision or purpose statement, my mission to carry out the vision, where I fit in the marketplace, what team members are necessary, financial projections, and organizational structure to accomplish it all. It doesn't matter whether you work for yourself or the city. You need a personal business plan! Your Roadmap to *RICHE$* is designed to assist you in developing this personalized plan!

Now, since I work for Tim Timmons, Inc., I must take on the position and responsibility of the CEO (Chief Executive Officer). You may call yourself Emperor, King, Monarch, President, Chief Cook & Bottle Washer—whatever refers to you as the one who is ultimately responsible.

Some people get nervous when I encourage this step, because they think this might take away some sort of authority from their relationship with God. I see the Creator-God as God! He doesn't want the position of CEO or President of your life. That would be a

demotion! He's God and you're not! Your job is to be the best manager of your giftedness that you can be!

Minding Your Own Riches—NO MATTER WHAT?

Remember the map marker that said, "It's not what happens to
you, but how you handle what happens to you that matters most!"
There is a tendency inside all of us to think that we have been dealt a
short hand or are uniquely handicapped in some way. Therefore, you
may think that you have an excuse not to be effective or successful.

Let's take a look at some of the hands that were dealt to some
very successful people. Some of the world's greatest men and women
have been saddled with disabilities and adversities, but have man-
aged to overcome them. Cripple him and you have a Sir Walter
Scott. Lock him in a prison cell and you have a John Bunyan. Bury
him in the snows of Valley Forge and you have a George Washington. Raise him in abject poverty and you have an Abraham Lincoln.
Subject him to bitter religious prejudice and you have a Benjamin
Disraeli. Strike him down with infantile paralysis and he becomes a
Franklin D. Roosevelt. Burn him so severely in a schoolhouse fire
that the doctors say he will never walk again and you have a Glenn
Cunningham, who set a world's record in 1934 for running a mile in
4 minutes, 6.7 secs. Deafen a genius composer and you have a Ludwig
van Beethoven. Have him or her born black in a society filled with
racial discrimination and you have a Booker T. Washing., a Harriet
Tubman, a Marian Anderson, or a George Washington Carver. Make
him the first child to survive in a poor Italian family of eighteen
children and you have an Enrico Caruso. Have him born of parents
who survived a Nazi concentration camp, paralyze him from the waist
down when he is four and you have an incomparable concert violin-

ist, Itzhak Perlman. Call him a slow learner, "retarded," and write him off as ineducable and you have an Albert Einstein.

Now, what's your excuse for not making the most of your life?

I love the following map marker about the caterpillar. May it be indelibly printed into your psyche as it is in mine.

Map Marker #33

Unfortunately, much of the time
we're like the caterpillar,
who watches a butterfly fly by
and says to himself:
"You'll never get me up in one of those things."

Chapter 3

What *RICHE$* Do You Want?

For over 32 years I have had the privilege of speaking to audiences of all sizes and proportions and counseling people from all walks of life. This has provided an amazing benefit to me that was impossible to see from the beginning of my career. I have been bombarded with questions!

These questions came from every angle—some hostile, some seeking, many interested to learn, and others out of desperation. Little did I know how valuable these questions were to me. Since I have a passion to empower people and a compassion for people growing through their difficulties, those questions became the primary connection I have had to fulfill my passion and compassion with them. You see, my entire life has been working on and answering life questions. All of my speaking and writing has been the results of these questions and answers.

Most everything that is good and genuine that comes forth from you will come from a well-placed question. The power of the question must not be overlooked. I have learned more about me—what

I feel, what I think and believe—through either someone asking me a question or from questioning myself.

In fact, this is precisely how I come up with my material for a weekly message at New Community. When I am speaking through a series, I work on a sub-question each week within the larger question of the series. Most nights I go to sleep with a question in mind and awaken to the answer or the way to find the answer.

Proper questioning can change your life! In a counseling session with a couple about a month ago the husband kept protesting that he felt he had never gotten what he wanted out of the marriage. He said this so many times that I finally asked him, "What is it that you want in this marriage?" He sat there, stunned, and after a long period of silence, said, "I don't know what I want!" Think of it! He's about to leave his wife of 18 years because he never gets what he wants and when questioned about it, he's stumped for an answer!

LIVING IN YOUR MIND'S EYE

When you work with your life questions, there are three major benefits that will come your way. First, *you will have thought through many of the life issues.* As we discussed in the last chapter, your mind is a powerful tool to make changes in your personness. Here is another way to use your mind. Thinking things through! It is said that only 5% think, 15% think they think, and 80% would rather die than think! This approach to life sets you up to live your life more effectively. Believe me, very few people in this world think things through before reacting to them.

Second, *you will be prepared to be proactive in these and similar life situations.* Once you've processed life issues you are then prepared to live your life on purpose—to be proactive rather than reactive! Most of life's problems arise out of our acting or reacting without thinking or without thinking it through. This kind of preparation is invaluable and allows you to act wisely in all that you do.

Third, *you will have the privilege of assisting others in getting through their life issues.* Now that you have processed and prepared yourself with respect to how to handle life issues, you move into an enviable position. You now have something to share with others and they want it. You move into a mentor status in the life issues you have processed.

The processing of your mind, the preparation for your actions, and the privilege of passing your wisdom on to others places you out in front of most of the rest of the world in a leadership role.

Map Marker #86

In the kingdom of the blind,
the one-eyed man is king!

Learn to ask yourself questions and seek out the answers! Always have a pad or notebook to capture those questions and answers, because they will become vital in handling your life in the weeks and years ahead.

Instead of living life by the seat of your pants, you'll be living in your mind's eye.

HOW DO YOU SPELL <u>RICHE$</u>

Years ago I did the writing on a major project about riches. During that entire experience I searched for a way to tie all of the riches together into one simple bundle, but could never figure anything out. I grappled with the question, "What are the primary riches that everyone wants and needs?" for several months! Then one day on an early morning I finally came to an answer. As soon as I reached my car I randomly wrote them down and throughout the rest of that day these riches began to jell into a nice package.

In the first draft I listed relationships, self-esteem, profession, health, finances, and spiritual. Then I received the answer to my question in a flood! The answer is **RICHE$** in the form of an acrostic—seven riches for you to pick up and possess as your own!

    R represents your **RELATIONAL RICHES!**
    I represents your **INTELLECTUAL RICHES!**
    C represents your **CAREER RICHES!**
    H represents your **HEALTH RICHES!**
    E represents your **EMOTIONAL RICHES!**
    $ represents your **FINANCIAL RICHES!**
    __ represents your **SPIRITUAL RICHES!**
    R—I—C—H—E—$

What Do YOU Really WANT?

To get to the question of "What do you want?" let's first lay some groundwork with respect to your basic reason for living and then we'll examine each of the seven riches in the chapters that follow.

In order to answer what riches you really want, you must go straight to the core of your being. At this core is your purpose for living. Your purpose in life is written on an inside label within your psyche. Only you know it and only you can read it!

Have you ever shared what you wanted to do in life with a friend or family member and been rebuffed for it? The response usually is, "Are you serious?" or "That could never happen!" or "You don't have enough education!" or "That would cost more than you'll ever have!" Your response to this reaction is normally to take your dreams underground and not share them any more. Or, you shut down the dreams altogether! This sort of scene is what stifles people from knowing and fulfilling their dreams. This is the kind of thing that has sent 'purpose in life' into the subconscious, at best!

Your purpose in life has the power to get you up in the morning and, more importantly, the power to take you across the goal line of your personal success. Without a purpose life can become overwhelming and depressing!

PURPOSE IN LIFE

Since the inner-label of your purpose can only be read by you, then how can you practically read it? I've been working with this in a practical way with various groups assisting them in discovering purpose for each of their lives. After developing 'wonderful' techniques to help each person read his/her inner-label, I quickly scrapped them all! There is a very simple way to read your inner-label. Hold on! It's almost overwhelmingly simple! JUST MAKE IT UP! That's it! Once you ask yourself the key question of purpose in life, you discover it as you are answering the question. It's amazing how well this works. Your purpose may not be as complete as you would like, at first. But take what you get and begin to build on your purpose statement. You will learn as you go!

HOW TO READ YOUR LABEL

Let's get on with 'making it up!' Use the following chart to assist you to target more clearly what your purpose in life is all about. What's the word you find most comfortable to fit in the blank of the following sentence: "My purpose in life is to _____ people." Just one simple verb is all it takes! Play with that for a while and think about the following list of words and see if one or more jumps out at you.

| teach | heal | organize | strengthen | polish |
| educate | elevate | support | enhance | refine |

inform	serve	expand	facilitate	awaken
empower	guide	nurse	stimulate	entertain
enlighten	assist	validate	discover	acknowledge
promote	prepare	cause	enroll	enable
liberate	influence	minister	coach	soothe
massage	mystify	encourage	referee	instruct
manage	help	challenge	paint	network

I want to _____ people. My purpose is to _____ people.

The next blank to fill in is with a description of who—individuals, groups, subsets, classes, types—who you want to serve or work with:

My purpose is to (word from above) people. Who are these people?

listeners	infirmed	wearers	patients	nations
children	teens	seniors	women	men
babies	choirs	audiences	sick	disabled
gifted	burned	wounded	kindergarten	poor
graduates	cancer	retired	immigrants	wealthy
toddlers	parents	brides	athletes	millionaires
boaters	artists	homeless	grandparents	inmates
viewers	armies	ethnics	singles	congregations

I want to (word from 1st group) (word from above).

The last blank to fill in is to describe the goal or result you wish to co-create with these people:

learn	earn	swim	appreciate	be responsible
be fit	love	rest	hear better	succeed
health	fun	happiness	wholeness	to explore
wealth	adventure	travel	prosperity	running events

(Action)   (People you want to serve)   (Goal)

My purpose is to _____ _____ _____.

The why and the where of your life combine to form the purpose of your life! Once you have the why (your purpose) and the where (your results) clearly in mind, you will change your life almost instantly to attract all you want. As your vision becomes clearer you will indeed be in a better position to pick up all of your riches and to possess them for your enjoyment!

Your purpose and results will change you as it transcends all of life's problems. Your problems! These problems begin either to take care of themselves or present a clear handle for you to handle them or they just don't matter in comparison to your all-inclusive purpose! A lofty purpose stated clearly contains the power to move mountains! It will help you to focus on the goals in picking up your riches and bring them into existence! And your goals will take you to your purpose like a rocket to the moon!

Write out your purpose statement and keep working on it.

I WANT TO (Action) (People you want to serve) (Result)!

Map Marker #19

Many are called, but few get up!

PURPOSE GUIDELINES

Your purpose is a calling on your life. I want to share with you several guidelines regarding your purpose that will continue to help you focus in on your inner-label and answer the call.

First, *purpose is not the same as goals.* Your purpose drives and

threads your goals together. By your purpose you know what you are to do and what you are not to do. Goals can be reached, but you are always leaning toward your purpose in life. There is no arrival-point; only a course or direction to your life!

Second, *your purpose must have a people connection.* A young man eager to fill in his purpose statement, quickly wrote out, "I want to market my financial product to the masses and make lots of money!" He was so proud that this seemed to fit in with his corporate business plan. but when I asked how this was going to positively affect people, he shrunk back into his chair with disappointment. The next week he had really worked on the people dimension of his purpose. His purpose ended up being very different from his job. His job would enable him to perform his purpose, but his job and his marketing plan is not his purpose in life.

Third, *your purpose may or may not have anything to do with your job. It pervades the* job. It gives your job and life meaning, possibly in connection with your job, but not necessarily. It's your life-force and drive that keeps you awake at night and gets you up in the morning with anticipation. I know many people who support themselves through their jobs, but are actively pursuing their purposes on the side.

Fourth, *your purpose will emerge out of your life-struggles and pain.* Those who have suffered from cancer inevitably have as their mission to give some sort of comfort and assistance to others fighting this same disease. This is true with abortions, abuses, disabilities, and other tragedies and losses people face. Brad Parks, who was paralyzed and left in a wheel chair the rest of his life, is the founder of Wheel Chair Tennis and now golf and basketball. His life took on the purpose around the tragedy he personally experienced. People with a rough childhood work with children and so on.

Fifth, *you never retire from your purpose.* It's your life! You are here on the planet to fulfill your purpose, until you die. Your purpose is your ultimate mission in life and you are tied to it, until you are relieved of your duties by death.

Sixth, *your purpose will continually be revised as you go*. It is made out of patchwork experiences—the latest is added on as you go.

Seventh, when you are on track with your God-stamped purpose, your Creator opens up all His power toward you and the fulfillment of your purpose. I am convinced that success is defined as being and doing all that you were created to be and to do. If this definition is accurate, then the power of your Creator is turned on with the performance of your purpose.

However you define God, there is no doubt that there is evidence of more and more that is supernatural out there in our daily lives. One of the most staggering studies has been led by a medical doctor, Larry Dossey. Without a religious twist, he has shown conclusively that prayer to God on behalf of another person makes a positive difference in the healing process of the patient.

Map Marker #24

Your Creator wants your success—to be and to do
all that He created you to be and to do!
Work in sync with Him as if He's your partner.
Work out of sync with Him
and you don't have a prayer!

Use the listing of terms and the guidelines to determine as best you can your purpose in life. No matter how rough it comes out in your first draft, write it down. Work with it, until you are able to make it better and more precise. You'll know when you are on the right track!

The biggest problem you face right now is the temptation to read on and not actually work on your purpose. This is a terrible mistake! Do it now!

To skip this crucial step before examining the riches is like the man who prayed constantly to God that he would win the lottery. He bargained with God, offering sizable splits of the winnings. He was so persistent and insistent that God appeared to him in the form of an angel right in the middle of one of his most sincere prayers. "God, please give a break. Let me win just this once!" God quickly replied, "Give me a break. At least, buy a ticket!"

I am convinced that we get so off-track with our lives that not even the Creator, Himself, can do anything to turn us around!

Once you have come to grips with your purpose in life, you are ready to more fully examine each of the 7 maps that lead to total satisfaction . . .

Map Marker #39

You can have anything you want, but not everything!

Chapter 4

Map #1—Relational *RICHE$!*

The primary objective of chapters 4 through 10 is to define each of the 7 riches and suggest practical steps for picking them up. To be most effective in picking up your personal riches, work the **Roadmap to _RICHE$_ Workbook**. Take the diagnostic tests and personalize the riches for yourself! Do this and you will produce a most rare and practical document—your personal business plan on how to live your life most successfully!

In order to examine each of the riches I want to use the same format throughout. First, the basic problem. Second, the most relevant principles. Third, several suggestions for you to pick up these riches for yourself.

I. THE RELATIONAL RICHES PROBLEM . . .

Being masters of surfacey relationships, we have created a desperate problem—a loss of intimacy! Everyone wants it, all of the 'shrinks' talk about it, the movies sell it, the pornographers counterfeit it, the 'self-help' books promise it, but *very few actually experience it! It's so alluring and yet so illusive!* The most frustrating aspect of the search for intimacy may be that you can't pursue it as a direct goal; you can reach it only as the by-product of your genuine willingness to be open with yourself and others!

The struggle for intimacy is painful. If the pain from relational failures doesn't put a halt to intimacy, then the painful fear of a new relationship will. Relationships demand active interest and maintenance or death is inevitable.

Relationships are extremely powerful! They can drag you down to despair or boost you toward your greatest fulfillment. When relationships work, life seems to work best, even in the worst of times. This is at the very core of your relational riches!

YOU NEED THE EGGS!

One of my favorite statements made concerning relationships was Woody Allen's award-winning film, *Annie Hall*. Its message was: relationships are difficult, painful, and much of the time they seem irrational, but you still need them. Woody Allen concluded his film in an uncharacteristic move by looking directly into the camera and telling the story about the woman who thought she was a chicken. Her husband went to see a psychiatrist for some help in dealing with his wife's problem. After he had explained his wife's behavior to the doctor, the doctor said, "That's ridiculous! Why don't you tell her she's not a chicken?" The man immediately responded, "I can't do that!" "Why?" the doctor asked. "Because I need the eggs!" *Relationships are difficult, but 'you need the eggs' for the nurturing and growing of your own personness!*

In a very helpful book, *Changes That Heal* (Zondervan Publishing House, 1992), Henry Cloud speaks to the importance of relationships by using the term, bonding. He says that bonding is the ability to establish an emotional attachment to another person. It's the ability to relate to another on the deepest level. When you

*Map #1—Relational **RICHE$**!* 6 5

experience this bond, you are able to share your deepest thoughts, dreams, and feelings with no fear that you will be rejected by the other.

Cloud refers to the most recent research that has shown "that a lack of bonding can affect one's ability to recover from an entire range of physical illness, including cancer, heart attack, and stroke. . . . evidence in the field of cardiology has shown that the nature of a patient's emotional ties drastically affects whether or not this patient will get heart disease. Experiments have shown that a patient's blood chemistry changes when that patient has a bitter thought. Doctors are now including, in their treatment of patients, training in becoming more loving and trusting. A person's ability to love and connect with others lays the foundation for both psychological and physical health. This research illustrates the when you are in a loving relationship, a bonded relationship, we are alive and growing. On the other hand, when you are isolated, you are dying a slow death.

II. THE RELATIONAL RICHES PRINCIPLES . . .

Healthy relationships are the primary ingredient for a good self-image. Many studies have shown that self-image is not related to family wealth, social class, father's occupation, education, geographical living area, or always having a mother at home. It comes from the quality of the relationships that exist between a person and those who play a significant role in his life. Whenever someone says, "I'm inadequate," he is not only commenting on his self-image, but also on the quality of his relationships that helped to mold his self-image.

Cultivating relationships is absolutely necessary for your psychological well-being, but there's a basic problem which constantly works against you!

Map Marker #171

Left to themselves—things tend to go from bad to worse!

Unfortunately, relationships are no exception to this life principle! The second law of thermodynamics states that everything is disintegrating, and that's also true in relationships. Contrary to popular opinion, relationships do not work out by themselves. If they're left to themselves, they disintegrate! Communication tends to break down when it isn't cultivated, and that produces all sorts of repressed thoughts and feelings. It usually doesn't take long before this repression builds up a festering of anger and resentment. This results in what I call a pressure-cooker lifestyle! If the lid on the pressure-cooker were ever opened, the repressed ugliness might surely seep out. Therefore, the pressure-cooker lifestyle relates primarily at the surface level. In order for you to cultivate love relationships, you must break the barrier (and habit) of surface relationships. You must fight against the second law of thermodynamics in your relationships!

RICHES OR WRECKAGE?

If you don't make the conscious choice to pick up your relational riches, your life is certain to be filled with relational wreckage—relationship after relationship that didn't work. In fact, the wreckage doesn't consist of just failed relationships, but a long list of damaged and bruised people—including you! This wreckage is strewn all over our society. Families, communities, corporations, civic, political, and religious organizations are filled with this wreckage!

*Map #1—Relational **RICHE$!***   **67**

To minimize leaving wreckage in your path you must make some choices that all have to do with choosing a context that promotes growth . . .

Choice #1—Growth or Stagnation?

Choose growth over stagnation—non-growth! Growth happens every time you break through a wall of frustration, work your way through a difficult trial, discipline yourself to do what you don't want to do or follow-through on what you started.

To choose stagnation is to decide on certain destruction! You must take the painful risk of growth at every turn of your life.

Choice #2—Accountability or Enablement?

Choose accountability over enablement! Within the context of faithful family and friends accountability always contributes to personal growth. Even though accountability can be a painful choice, it is a freeing choice. Just as a train must remain on the set of tracks in order to enjoy the freedom to be a train, so humans have been created to operate best running on certain people tracks. Friends and family who have your best at heart bring more growth and healing along with this function of accountability.

It's also interesting to note that when Jesus was asked what the greatest of the commandments was, he immediately said, "Love God with all of your heart . . . and love your neighbor as yourself!" He based all of the commandments upon the love relationship you have with the God of gods and with your fellow-man!

To choose enablement is to choose a life full of distraction! When you allow yourself to be enabled by family and friends, all of the focus is taken off of you and your life and pointed toward everyone and anyone else. Within the context of enablement you don't have to face any responsibility and therefore personal growth cannot happen!

Choice #3—Supportive or Competitive?

Choose supportive over competitive! Within the context of family and faithful friends cultivate the supportive relationships. Life's too short to feel you have to compete at every level with everyone all of the time. You need supportive family and friends in your life who truly care for your well-being and success. It's within this context that you realize you are not alone in your plight in life. You need to know that you are not the only one going through whatever you are going through. Misery not only loves company, but you can find strength there, too.

To choose the competitive is to choose discouragement and disappointment most of the time! When you compare yourself with others you will either be filled with pride, set up for a fall, or filled with depression, already experiencing the fall.

Choice #4—Interaction or Loning it?

Choose interaction over loning it! You will not experience any significant growth in a vacuum. It's only as you interact with others that you experience life to its fullest. Through the onslaught of various circumstances in life you may find yourself in an undesirable situation that you would not have chosen. But it's at this point that you have the option to choose your way out of this bad predicament. For example, you may not choose to be lonely. When a loved one dies or leaves, you find yourself in a pile of loneliness. Now, you didn't choose this loneliness, but you do choose to stay there or get out!

To choose loning it is to choose disconnection! Disconnection cuts you off from the primary flow of life and healing. When you choose to be disconnected from others, you send a clear signal that there is something wrong in your life. This is what is meant in the anonymous movement as "you are as sick as your secrets."

Map #1—Relational **RICHE$!** 69

Most intimate of all—THE SAFE PLACE!

Nowhere are relational riches more deeply experienced than in the intimate, male-female relationship. No matter where I speak in the world and no matter the audience, the energy level dramatically rises to a new level when I mention the subject of male-female intimacy. Although this relationship is riddled with failure and pain, everyone is looking for some sliver of hope for how to make it work better!

A hippo and a butterfly fell deeply in love. However, in their emotional bliss they never once considered that this kind of union between and hippo and a butterfly had never ever occurred before! Family and friends gently urged them to consult the wise, old owl about this potential problem.

When they explained their marital intentions to the owl, he sat very still for a very long time. Then the owl smiled and pronounced it a good idea. "Why not? All that has to be done is that you Mr. Hippo must become a butterfly and all will be wonderful! Go for it!" The hippo and the butterfly were so surprised at his enthusiastically, positive answer and skipped off into the forest without any hesitation. They were so very happy!

But then, the hippo stopped and wondered, "How? How do I become a butterfly?" With that question they made their way back to talk to the owl again!

"Mr. Owl! We appreciate your encouragement and approval, but, tell us, how can I, a huge hippo, become a butterfly?" Without any hesitation the owl said, "How should I know? I only set policy. I'm not into implementation!"

This scenario reminds me of many of the marriages I've witnessed. People plan for where they will live, how to drive to and from their home, how to pay for their lifestyle, but how to live is taken for granted. Somehow this dimension will 'work out'! There is so much excitement on the wedding day, but very little thought and preparation for implementing a healthy relationship. When I perform a wedding ceremony, I begin with the following map marker . . .

Map Marker #93

"All weddings are happy; it's the living together afterward that causes all of the trouble!"

I've never seen a bride and groom at the altar on their wedding day without great anticipation and excitement. When asked if they 'do', they each say, maybe with a degree of nervousness for the moment, 'I do!' No one pauses in doubt and no one says 'I don't!'

Getting back to THE SAFE PLACE!

Thousands of couples have shared their stories with me and most of them remember the exact day and even the words that were said when they lost the safe place in their relationship. When you think about it, it's within this most intimate relationship that you ought to feel safe. However, the safe place is a rare experience for most couples. Most seem to go through the 3 stages of a male/female relationship . . .

Map Marker #23

The 3 Stages of a male/female relationship!
First, they believe they have found the IDEAL.
Second, they experience a difficult ORDEAL.
Third, then they start looking for a NEW DEAL.

Map #1—Relational **RICHE$!** 7 1

The safe place is what everyone is looking for in a relationship. As I see it, there are four fundamental dimensions of the safe place. Let's take a brief look at each one . . .

S—Shelter!

The safe place is a shelter—a protection from the stresses and strains of life. This protection is both physical and psychological. Feeling safe from physical harm is fundamental in a relationship—free from all manner of abusive actions, words, and intimidation.

The psychological form of protection is the difficult to sustain. However, there is a way to go straight to the core of sheltering one another. It is found in understanding and acceptance. Feeling understood may be the strongest demonstration of love. Nothing feels better than to be understood—to be known and still accepted!

A—Affirmation!

The safe place is affirmation! Building upon the protection of the shelter positive affirmation of who you are is most powerful. Affirmation is being a good finder and communicating what you have found. No one on earth can stand up against a barrage of genuine, positive affirmation.

Now don't get the wrong idea. Affirmation is not simply complimenting your partner, when you like what he/she did. Affirmation is most powerful when you point out the differences, not just the similarities or agreements. When affirmation goes to this extent, you are free to be all that you were created to be and to do! This is the safe place!

F—Friendship!

A few years ago I had the privilege of teaching a group of about 100 singles. It was a weekly experience that lasted for over a year!

While struggling with their questions and needs, I stumbled upon an insight that has proven to be exceptionally powerful in the lives of men and women alike.

Most singles date around looking for that special person and dance around the big C word—COMMITMENT. Commitment, then, becomes a thing to be achieved, a thing to be grown, and a thing that is overanalyzed, but greatly feared. I realized that this is all backwards! When you start dating someone, why not begin the relationship (early in the relationship) with a commitment? This is a commitment to friendship! Make the commitment to be a good friend. Make the commitment that nothing that you do in this relationship will violate your friendship with this person. Not your behavior. Not your attitude. Not your communication. Not any level of intimacy! *Not even your decision to marry will interfere with your commitment to friendship!* Approaching a relationship in this way would have people actually marrying their friends! What a concept! Believe me, it's more difficult to marry someone and then try to make him your friend later!

A safe place in an intimate relationship means that you enjoy a close, trusted friendship with this person. This means having fun together—building a reservoir of shared experiences. It's the joy of sharing your fears, anger, guilt, goals, dreams, and life's challenges. It's having a close team member who is always covering your back! The entire dynamic is the spirit of completing one another rather than competing with one another!

E—Empowerment!

The safe place is empowerment! When you understand that the first step toward intimacy is working on your uniqueness, then you want that intimate relationship to encourage that uniqueness. You want your significant other to empower you toward becoming all that you were created to be and to do. You want your relationship to

Map #1—Relational **_RICHE$!_** 73

set you free to be YOU! You want your relationship to make you a better YOU! The safe place is always empowering and avoids all that might disempower!

WHY ARE WOMEN SO WEIRD & MEN SO STRANGE?

Over the last 30 years more than 90% of all Americans declared themselves dedicated to the ideal of two people sharing a life and a home together. Why, then, does the battle of the sexes still rage on?

I'm convinced that the battle lingers on because the most basic principle of the sexes continues to be violated: difference! We strive for equality (which is desirable) and achieve sameness (which is destructive)! Men and women are incurably different. And it's only when you understand that difference that you are free to be complementary to one another.

The only possible way to end this great sexual war is to sharpen the focus on the complementary difference between men and women. As I have carefully studied this difference I have come to a basic conclusion about men and women. *Women are weird!* And, *men are very strange!*

Do you love me?

A woman asks her man, "Do you love me?" (It's 8:00). "Are you sure?" (8:10). "You really do?" (8:15). "You do, huh?" (8:20). In the meantime, her man is thinking (and maybe saying), "I told you I loved you when I married you and it's still in effect until I take it back!" Now that's a major difference!

That same kind of difference is illustrated when a couple receives an invitation to a party. The woman's response is, "What shall I wear?" and the man's, "How can I get out of this one?"

Men and women approach life from completely different perspectives or different planets as John Gray so ably point out—Mars and Venus! Check out this common scenario of the difference . . .

Let's say a guy named Roger is attracted to a woman named Elaine.

He asks her out to a movie; she accepts; they have a pretty good time. A few nights later he asks her out to dinner, and again they enjoy themselves. They continue to see each other regularly, and after a while neither one of them is seeing anybody else.

And then, one evening when they're driving home, a thought occurs to Elaine, and, without really thinking, she says it aloud: "Do you realize that, as of tonight, we've been seeing each other for exactly six months?"

And then there is silence in the car. To Elaine, it seems like a very loud silence. She thinks to herself: Gee, I wonder if it bothers him that I said that. Maybe he's been feeling confined by our relationship; maybe he thinks I'm trying to push him into some kind of obligation that he doesn't want, or isn't sure of.

Roger is thinking: Gosh. Six months.

Elaine is thinking: But, hey, I'm not so sure I want this kind of relationship, either. Sometimes I wish I had a little more space, so I'd have time to think about whether I really want us to keep going the way we are, moving steadily toward . . . I mean, where are we going? Are we just going to keep seeing each other at this level of intimacy? Are we heading toward marriage? Toward children? Toward a lifetime together? Am I ready for that level of commitment? Do I really even know this person?

Roger is thinking: . . . so that means it was . . . let's see . . . February when we started going out, which was right after I had the car at the dealer's, which means let me check the odometer. . . Whoa! I am way overdue for an oil change here.

Elaine is thinking: He's upset. I can see it on his face. Maybe I'm reading this completely wrong. Maybe he wants more from our relationship, more intimacy, more commitment; maybe he has sensed-even before I sensed it-that I was feeling some reservations. Yes, I

Map #1—Relational **RICHE$!** 75

bet that's it. That's why he's so reluctant to say anything about his own feelings. He's afraid of being rejected.

Roger is thinking: And I'm gonna have them look at the transmission again. I don't care what those morons say, it's still not shifting right. And they better not try to blame it on the cold weather this time. What cold weather? It's 87 degrees out, and this thing is shifting like a garbage truck, and I paid those incompetent thieves $600.

Elaine is thinking: He's angry. And I don't blame him. I'd be angry, too. I feel so guilty, putting him through this, but I can't help the way I feel. I'm just not sure.

Roger is thinking: They'll probably say it's only a 90-day warranty. That's exactly what they're going to say, the rats.

Elaine is thinking: maybe I'm just too idealistic, waiting for a knight to come riding up on his white horse, when I'm sitting right next to a perfectly good person, a person I enjoy being with, a person I truly do care about, a person who seems to truly care about me. A person who is in pain because of my self-centered, schoolgirl romantic fantasy.

Roger is thinking: Warranty? They want a warranty? I'll give them a warranty. I'll take their warranty and stick it right up their . . .

"Roger," Elaine says aloud.

"What?" says Roger, startled.

"Please don't torture yourself like this," she says, her eyes beginning to brim with tears. "Maybe I should never have . . . I feel so" (She breaks down, sobbing.)

"What?" says Roger.

"I'm such a fool," Elaine sobs. "I mean, I know there's no knight. I really know that. It's silly. There's no knight, and there's no horse."

"There's no horse?" says Roger.

"You think I'm a fool, don't you?" Elaine says.

"No!" says Roger, glad to finally know the correct answer.

"It's just that . . . It's that I . . . I need some time," Elaine says.

(There is a 15-second pause while Roger, thinking as fast as he can, tries to come up with a safe response. Finally he comes up with one that he thinks might work.)

"Yes," he says.

(Elaine, deeply moved, touches his hand.)

"Oh, Roger, do you really feel that way?" she says.

"What way?" says Roger.

"That way about time," says Elaine.

"Oh," says Roger. "Yes."

(Elaine turns to face him and gazes deeply into his eyes, causing him to become very nervous about what she might say next, especially if it involves a horse. At last she speaks.)

"Thank you, Roger," she says.

"Thank you," says Roger.

Then he takes her home, and she lies on her bed, a conflicted, tortured soul, and weeps until dawn, whereas when Roger gets back to his place, he opens a bag of Doritos, turns on the TV, and immediately becomes deeply involved in a rerun of a tennis match between two Czechs he never heard of. A tiny voice in the far recesses of his mind tells him that something major was going on back there in the car, but he is pretty sure there is no way he would ever understand what, and so he figures it's better if he doesn't think about it. (This is also Roger's policy regarding world hunger.)

The next day Elaine will call her closest friend, or perhaps two of them, and they will talk about this situation for six straight hours. In painstaking detail, they will analyze everything she said and everything he said, going over it time and time again, exploring every word, expression, and gesture for nuances of meaning, considering every possible ramification. They will continue to discuss this sub-

*Map #1—Relational **RICHE$!*** 7 7

ject, off and on, for weeks, maybe months, never reaching any definite conclusions, but never getting bored with it, either.

Meanwhile, Roger, while playing racquetball one day with a
mutual friend of his and Elaine's, will pause just before serving, frown,
and say: "Norm, did Elaine ever own a horse?"

Do you get it? Women are weird and men are so strange!

First Things First!

Priorities are for people. We seem to always complain that our
days are few, and acting as though there would be no end to them!
You will never *find* time for anything. If you want time you must
make it—or take it from what you are given. You are given the same
amount of time as everyone else in the world. The challenge is how
will you invest it!

Priorities refer to how you prefer to spend or invest your time—
the quality dimension! A priority is a preference of one activity over
another and of spending time with one person over another. In this
pressure-cooker world one of the greatest battles occurs on the battle-
field of priorities. It's not always choosing what is good or what is
bad, but it's a choice of what is wise versus what is foolish. It's a
battle between that which is good and that which is best!

Map Marker #113

The 'good' is the greatest enemy of the 'best.'

You need priorities in order to make decisions that will produce
peace instead of pressure. Some of the most intense pressures in life
are created by your inability to say no. The tension is great. Either you

are intimidated into saying yes to something that warranted a no or you say no to someone and carry the guilt for turning them down.

By setting your priorities you will free yourself from the unnecessary pressures. I used to feel guilty for taking a day off or for turning down a speaking opportunity or another counseling session. But not anymore! I have a freedom to say no, based on my priorities.

One word of caution before listing the key priorities. You may feel that you have only to conquer this problem of priorities once and for all. The truth is that you will have to fight continually to maintain your priorities. Believe me, it is a daily fight! Once you think your priorities are moving along smoothly and nothing can detour or distract you. And then the phone rings! That's all it takes! One phone call with someone pulling on your time, forcing you into making new choices on how you will spend these precious moments. You can easily be pulled back into living your life under "the tyranny of the urgent."

Here are the 5 basic priorities that have been most helpful to me and to thousands of people with whom I've shared them over the years . . .

1. *Your relationship with your Creator*! I define success as being and doing all that you were created to be and to do. I find it most helpful to stop and realize that there is a God out there and I am not Him!

2. *Your relationship with your spouse*! Men tend to slip their vocation into this slot, while women frequently place their children here.

3. *Your children*! You may fail miserably as a parent in the area of discipline, being either too permissive or too authoritarian, and still succeed if there is a healthy relationship that has been cultivated. Although priorities are referring to qual-

*Map #1—Relational **RICHE$!*** 79

ity of time more than quantity of time, be careful not to use that as a cop-out. Relationships take time. You'll never regret the time you have taken with your children!

4. *Your vocation!* Your bills must be paid, but if this priority is all-consuming and damaging to the higher priorities, you will incur greater bills than you could imagine!

5. *Your social relationships*—those outside your home or vocation! This would include friends, neighbors, and extended family.

These priorities—your Creator, spouse, children, vocation and social relationships—determine where you spend your quality time. With this kind of grid it's easier to emphasize those priorities which are at the top of your list. When you neglect the higher priorities in your life, you set all kinds of time-bombs that will go off at the most inopportune times in the weeks, months and years ahead! Defuse them right now by working on your priorities!

III. THE RELATIONAL RICHES PICKUP . . .

Map Marker #44

Life is a series of responsibilities
lived out in the context of relationships!

Relationships do provide the basic context for all of life and happiness! Relationships provide the seeds of self-esteem, the support within friendships, the strength of family, the soul of intimacy, and the soil for learning. They are sometimes painful, but always necessary for a life that is growing, succeeding and healing.

Here are four suggested steps to help you pick up your relational riches:

STEP 1—Discover your poverty without people!

You must see and admit your need for people. You are not an island unto yourself. You are not self-sufficient.

If you were to draw your lifeline along a horizontal time line— and make the lifeline go above the horizontal time line during growth periods and below it during the non-growth periods—in most cases the growth periods would directly correspond to the times there were significant relationships with one or more people. This supports a study that pinpointed the difference between happy and unhappy people. It concluded that the single most impressive difference between the two groups was that happy people were successfully involved with others, while unhappy people were not!

When you are in your darkest moments, your worst trials and troubles, other people turn out to be the specific answers to your prayers for help. I have seen this my own experience over and over. In fact, it is in the midst of your toughest times that people are revealed as to their value in your life. Although people cause pain, people become the primary pain relievers in your life! *Don't waste your pain!* Use your pain and the problems you face as instant triggers to remind you that you need people! And, much to my surprise, the people who turn out to be the most helpful are not necessarily the 'cool' and 'lovely' people in my world. Notice that you are not to discover your poverty without certain people, but without people in general.

STEP 2—Distinguish everyone as your peer!

This step follows directly on the heels of the first. Once you discover your need for people, you must distinguish everyone as your peer. View everyone as having a special message, a significant contri-

*Map #1—Relational **RICHE$!*** 81

bution to make in yours and others lives. Each one of us has a genetic code (DNA) which distinguishes each person from all others. Your genetic code contains the primary instructions as to the color of your eyes and hair, your physical build, whether or not you'll be folically challenged, and marks you with a basic purpose in life through which you make a positive contribution to others! In order to take advantage of everyone's contribution, you must distinguish everyone as your peer. *Don't wreck the potential of the people in your life!*

Map Marker #211

If Ben Franklin had tried to be a General
and George Washington had tried to be an inventor,
we'd be living in a British colony without electricity!

STEP 3—Determine that life must begin with you!

Note the progression of these steps! First, you discover your poverty without people, then you distinguish everyone as your peer, but you can't wait for others to go first. You must develop them yourself! *Don't wait for people to do it for you!* Initiate the expression of your uniqueness and contribute to those around you.

There is a fascinating dynamic in the midst of your initiation. When you show love toward someone, you receive it back. This is not an experience of karma. In karma, you send out something good and good returns later. In this dynamic, you initiate something good toward another and you receive it back—at the very moment you are giving it out! So, when you love someone, you receive love at the same time. When you forgive, you are forgiven. When you show compassion, you receive compassion. (You'll see this dynamic more fully expressed later!)

STEP 4—Discipline yourself to maintain!

The most common flaw within the human condition is inconsistency. Most people are good in the crisis, but not so good in the continual! Once you discover your poverty without people, distinguish everyone as your peer, and determine that life must begin with you, you are faced with one of the most difficult responsibilities of all. You must discipline yourself to maintain! Develop the habit of connecting with people. *Don't wash your people prosperity down the drain*!

Discipline has been defined as love for that which you are disciplining. If you discipline your children, you are loving them. If you discipline your self, you are loving yourself. So, when you discipline yourself to plug into people, you are loving yourself! And, when you are loving yourself in this way, you are continuing to pick up your own relational riches!

Map Marker #28

A friend is someone who leaves you
with all of your freedom intact,
yet obliges you to be fully what you are.

Chapter 5

Map #2—Intellectual *RICHES!*

There is a theory of human behavior that says people subconsciously retard their own intellectual growth. They come to rely on clichés and habits. Once they reach the age of their own personal comfort with the world, they stop learning and their mind runs on idle for the rest of their days. They may progress organizationally, they may be ambitious and eager, and they may even work night and day. But they learn no more. The bigoted, the narrow-minded, the stubborn, and the perpetually optimistic have all stopped learning.

Map Marker #26

When I work, I work hard.
When I sit, I sit loose.
And when I think, I fall asleep!

I. THE INTELLECTUAL RICHES PROBLEM . . .

Although you face many problems as you make your way through life, there is an ever-present residue of stress that continually wears your system down. The stress mess! There are two extreme approaches to handling life an its stresses. One extreme says *life is always being on top of the pile*—filled with optimism—positive with rarely a thought of the negative at all. When asked, "How are you doing?", people in this extreme say, "Super! Fantastic! Couldn't be better!" (Yet even though they have a big smile on the outside, they may be dying on the inside.) In this extreme you have to be on top all the time—always enthusiastic, all of the time! This person must be on something!

The other extreme says life is always being underneath the pile—filled with pessimism—always dwelling on the negative, with rarely a thought of the positive! "Life is getting worse," warn those in this extreme, "and it isn't likely to get any better." People in this extreme have faces long enough to eat pop-corn out of milk bottle! Instead of exciting people about life (as do those who are on top of the pile), they're embalming people—preparing everyone for death!

Both of these extremes are wrong! Life is not always being on top of the pile and neither is it always being underneath the pile. The position in which you find yourself with life's onslaught will constantly differ. You may be on top of a pile or underneath. You may try to go around or shovel through. But no matter where you are or what you're doing, you can't avoid the stress. *Life is full of piles!*

The Stress Mess!

Western thinkers divide man into body, mind, and spirit. Physicians treat the body, psychologists and psychiatrists deal with the mind, and the clergy attend to the spirit. In the past, the three areas were most often dealt with separately, but now that we have entered the age of stress, we must deal with the whole person simultaneously.

Map #2—Intellectual RICHE$!　　85

One standard medical text estimates that 50 to 80 percent of all diseases have their origins in stress. Stress-induced disorders have long since replaced infectious disease as the most common maladies of people in the postindustrial nations.

During recent years, heart disorders, cancer, arthritis, and all sorts of respiratory diseases have become so prominent in the clinics of the United States, Western Europe, and Japan, that they are known as "the afflictions of civilization." Their prevalence stems from poor diet, pollution, and most important, the increased stress of modern society.

The wear and tear of stress is part of the cost of living—no one can avoid it. But for most of us the price has risen too high to pay as we're exposed to the explosion of the time bombs. You face more daily pressures, such as the unrelenting demands of time, than anyone has at any other time in history. The effect can be devastating!

Some people are only vaguely aware of the toll stress is taking on them. Others are acutely aware of it and they have the medical bills to prove it! Things such as financial difficulties, legal entanglements, a business setback, or a death in the family are obvious sources of the stress mess. However, not all stress arises from negative events. Positive occurrences, such as a marriage, a desired pregnancy, a promotion, an outstanding achievement, or even a simple vacation can produce stress. Both winning a lottery and getting a ticket for speeding can make your heart pound, your stomach churn, and your palms sweat. Our bodies exert themselves in much the same way to cope with both desired situations and dreaded events.

The Body's M.O. During Stress

Your body's modus operandi or manner of operation (M.O.) for defending itself against stressful situations is extremely complex. Whenever a desired or dreaded stress occurs, your mind rapidly classifies it and sets off an alarm system. Your nervous system takes over immediately and makes the necessary adjustments. Then your pulse rate soars and respiration is retarded. As your blood pressure rises, your heart works harder to distribute the excess supply of blood to the muscles and lungs. All processes in your alimentary canal cease; and your spleen contracts, sending its concentrated corpuscles to pre-designated areas. Adrenaline is excreted from the adrenal medulla; sugar is freed from the reserves in the liver; and literally thousands of other complex procedures occur instantaneously and automatically without you having to give them the slightest thought. This marvelous transformation, this M.O. protects and provides for you in the midst of your stress.

There's A Tiger Outside

You seldom face a saber-toothed tiger as your ancestors did. Rather, your defenses are more likely to be required for a chewing out by the boss or a score of less important situations which keep your body constantly on the alert. You are an organism prepared for fight, flight, or freeze, even when nothing is happening or is going to happen. You are actually stewing in your own juice that consists of excess adrenaline and other glandular secretions. Now, the stage is set for anything from a headache to a heart attack!

For most it doesn't require a stress of any magnitude to set off their alarm systems. A thought, a look, a TV program, or a train going by. The body's chemistry is so severely altered after its defenses are alerted that if no physical action is taken in time various physical or emotional symptoms may occur. It's like holding the accelerator of your car to the floor while keeping its gears in neutral or its brake on. Going nowhere, your body roars and races, using up its energy and wearing out its parts!

Add to the stress mess the context of difficult and complex relationships and the stress gets even more messy!

Map #2—Intellectual **RICHE$!**   8 7

The Stress Mess in the Underground

I'm convinced that most of the stress people experience isn't obvious, but having initially gone underground, it sneaks up later without warning to destroy. Sometimes this kind of stress only indirectly affects you and your life, but sometimes it may directly affect you and end your life!

The piles of debris from the many shock waves and shrapnel can't be escaped. It's all part of the human condition! However, you can do something about the damaging effects. The controlling factor in determining which effect stressful debris will have—healer or killer—is in the use of the mind!

There are so many cases of terminally ill people who have had an unanticipated recovery when they deeply desired to live, perhaps to experience a special event, such as the birth of a grandchild. In other cases fatally ill patients have hung on beyond all expectations, dying only after a significant event, such as the death of a spouse or a birthday. Whatever else may contribute to such miraculous occurrences or timely deaths, it's certain that a person's will to recover or remain alive has a decisive effect on what actually does happen. We are still in the beginning stages of understanding the power of your mind. King Solomon's words ring clearer today than ever before: "As a person thinks in his heart, so is he!"

Map Marker #91

As you think, you are.
As you think, you feel.
As you think, you do.

The intellectual riches problem is rooted in the stress mess! But you can sort out the stress mess with the right input—the right kind of thinking. In the recovery world there is a great term—STINKIN' THINKIN'! The challenge in life with respect to your mind is to learn how to overhaul it, so that you are getting the best effort from your most powerful computer. *By fueling your mind with the following intellectual riches principles, you set yourself up to have it all! You can clear up your faulty and fuzzy thinking, focus on your tasks, calm your anxieties, and effectively care for your inner soul!*

II. THE INTELLECTUAL RICHES PRINCIPLES . . .

David was one of the great kings of ancient Israel. He was a successful warrior and a gifted leader among his people. After his death, his son, Solomon found himself heir to the throne as a very young man. Solomon describes himself at that time as one who barely had enough savvy to know when to come in out of the rain. He saw himself as young, inexperienced and very naïve.

When God offered to give Solomon anything he wished, Solomon quickly answered well. He requested wisdom! God's response to Solomon's request is recorded in the Hebrew scriptures in the book of Kings and was very interesting.

God said, "Because you have asked this thing and have not asked for yourself long life, nor asked riches for yourself, nor have you asked for the life of your enemies, but you have asked for yourself discernment to understand justice, behold, I have done according to your words. Behold, I have given you a wise and discerning heart, so that there has been no one like you before you, nor shall one like you arise after you. I have also given you what you have not asked, both riches and honor, so that there will not be any among the kings like you all your days."

Map #2—Intellectual __RICHE$__!   89

When it comes to the most valuable of any kind of riches, wisdom must be listed right at the top. And, *wisdom is at the very core of intellectual riches*! To have wisdom does not mean to have knowledge or to know it all. So many have loads of knowledge, yet prove to be foolish. To have wisdom does not mean that you are smart in the traditional sense of the word. I'm sure you know lots of smart people who have not learned to major in wisdom.

Map Marker #139

To know what to do with what you know
is the essence of wisdom!

Fools Find It Difficult To Hide!

When studying the difference between that which is wise and that which is foolish, I ran across the following story. Dr. Leroy, the head psychiatrist at the local mental hospital, is examining patients to see if they're cured and ready to re-enter society. "So, Mr. Clark," the doctor says to one of his patients, "I see by your chart that you've been recommended for dismissal. Do you have any idea what you might do once you're released from the hospital?"

The patient thinks for a moment, then replies, "Well, I went to school for mechanical engineering. That's still a good field, good money there. But on the other hand, I thought I might write a book about my experience here in the hospital, what it's like to be a patient here. People might be interested in reading a book like that. In addition, I thought I might go back to college and study art history, which I've grown interested in lately."

Dr. Leroy nods and says, "Yes, those all sound like intriguing possibilities."

The patient replies, "And the best part is, in my spare time, I can go on being a TEAPOT."

Even The Wise Can Play The Part Of The Fool!

The Wise Man Dakhow was a very wise man wearing his signature beard about a foot long. One day, he was reading the "wisdom of the past ages" and came across a passage that said this: "Any beard longer than the man's fist below his chin is a sign of stupidity."

He became very concerned and took a good look at his beard, grabbed it in his hand just below his chin and measured. He realized than it was much longer than the standards for wisdom. So, he decided to take care of it immediately. He went near his oil burning lamp, held his beard in his fist and proceeds to burn off his excess beard over the flame. As his beard barely touched the flame it caught on fire burning his hand and the entire hair on his face!

He then cleaned up the ashes gracefully and returned to study, jotting a note next to what he had just read. Dakhow wrote in the margin: *This statement was experimented and proven to be true!*

Map Marker #151

It is wise to act wise, unless you're otherwise!

THE 7 PILLARS OF WISDOM!

I want to walk you through seven of the most powerful insights I've ever encountered! They were first penned by King Solomon in the book of Proverbs. The entire book is written to teach a young

Map #2—Intellectual __RICHE$__!   9 1

boy what kind of wisdom it takes to become a great king. Each of these seven pillars of wisdom contributes a major ingredient to the full definition of wisdom. To define wisdom without all of them is to have a partial picture of what wisdom is all about!

The seven pillars of wisdom are the most practical insights ever! These are not theories to be learned, but tenets to be lived out in real life. I see the seven pillars of wisdom as seven 'life affirmations' that can get you through any situation—any crisis, any challenge, any circumstance! In order to pick up your intellectual riches, you must get a handle on these seven pillars of wisdom for yourself. Personalize all seven of them—for life! Make them your personal life affirmations!

Not only are the seven pillars of wisdom—the life affirmations—most practical, I have found them to be most useful to view them as a plan for living your life most skillfully—most successfully! Let's examine each of these pillars.

We'll only be able to scratch the surface, but this will give you some further work to do on your own.

LIFE AFFRIMATION #1—FEAR OF THE LORD!

It was a cool, crisp Saturday afternoon and Mr. Marshall was busily installing a new television antenna on his roof. He was just about finished, hurrying to finish before the big game came on, when he slipped and began to fall. He slid down the roof, over the edge, and barely caught himself on the gutter. There he was dangling by his fingertips, two stories above the ground. In this difficult predicament he yelled, "Is there anybody down there who can help me?" Not a soul heard him. No one!

With no time to wait around for a someone to come along, he then looked up into the clouds and yelled, "Is there anybody up there who can help me?" At that precise instant, the clouds parted and a voice blared out, "BELIEVE AND LET GO!" In a total panic Mr. Marshall quickly glanced down again and then back up and shouted, "Is there anybody *else* up there who can help me?"

It's this kind of leap in the dark that typifies the popular thinking about anything to do with God. Believe and let go!

Without the Fear of the Lord You Have Only a Religious System

And no matter what flavor of religion you choose, most of them taste alike. Catholic, Protestant, Jew, Moslem and all their various spin-offs only seem to be offering more leaps in the dark. Unfortunately, so many of the most popular religions tend to be filled with 'add-ons' that are purely man-made and have little to do with God. Religious experience becomes a system of do's and don'ts—mostly don'ts! It's like trying to get to heaven on a six-foot ladder—you can only go six feet up!

As I was growing up, I was interested in knowing how I could get my ticket to get into heaven. My particular church had it all figured out. We had a list of do's and don'ts prominently displayed on the wall of our church. They were mostly negative. In looking over the list, I realized that many of them were my goals in life! Over the years I have discovered that I am not alone in my search and it is clear that many, if not most, have thrown the baby out with the bath when it comes to dealing with God.

Imagine that all of the leaders of the man-made religions and their cultish off-shoots were gathered into a great arena before God in heaven. God looks out among them and inquires, "Who do you say that I am?" One by one they each respond with their names and descriptions of him: "The Thetan of Thetans! The Source of Divine Energy! The Essence of All Consciousness! The Wholly Other! The Ground of Being! The Infinite Transcendent Emanation! The Spirit of All Life!" and so on, ad infinitum. Finally, after the last one was

Map #2—Intellectual __RICHE$!__   9 3

finished, God rubbed his chin and muttered a puzzled, "Huh???" Religion and religiosity are confusing! No, without the fear of the Lord you have only a religious system of do's and don'ts!

Without Fear of the Lord You Have Little Foundation for Values

Without the Fear of the Lord in our society we'd be living in a world filled with violence, corruption, self-centeredness, greed, envy and immorality at every level. We'd be living in a world without values! Wait a minute! That sounds just like the evening news!

We are living in a valueless society, because we are attempting to live without the Fear of the Lord. The lack of a rooted moral belief system—a system of values—is the deepest challenge to our survival as a society!

Every ethical belief and moral standard within our culture is in a constant state of disintegration. No matter what the belief or what the standard, they all pass through three very definite steps of disintegration. The first is: *"It all depends on how you look at it!"* Then, after thinking it over a little bit, the second step follows: *"It really doesn't' make any difference how you look at it!"* Finally, the realization of the third step hits: *"I don't think anybody knows how to look at it!"* The disintegration of values! No one seems to know 'how to look at it' any longer. Without the Fear of the Lord there is no adequate standard of right and wrong—a society without values!

Plugged or Unplugged?

Although I grew up under the strict teaching of the Fear of the Lord, it wasn't until I understood the concept of God as my Higher Power that I was able to embrace this affirmation and experience it in my daily life. At the same time I stumbled on a most profound, yet simple, principle.

Map Marker #13

Everything works best when it's plugged in!

And, everyone works best when he is plugged into his Creator! This is the dynamic principle of the Higher Power. In the recovery world, you would be hard-pressed to find anyone in the anonymous groups who would even think of living without their Higher Power. To do so would be certain destruction and death!

According to King Solomon the addition of the Fear of the Lord . . .

    . . . is the beginning of wisdom!
    . . . adds length to life!
    . . . is a fountain of life!
    . . . leads to life!
    . . . and humility bring wealth and honor and life!

Notice how the addition of the Fear of the Lord centers around the fullness of life itself! It brings a sense of satisfaction, a sense of security, and a sense of destiny and hope!

THE FEAR OF THE LORD?

So, what is the Fear of the Lord? In each of the seven pillars of wisdom I have discovered two fundamental dimensions that are vital to its understanding.

First, THE AWESOMENESS OF GOD! The Fear of the Lord is not to fear God with a sense of terror or to be exceptionally fearful. However, it does mean to view God with a sense of awe, a rever-

Map #2—Intellectual **RICHE$!**   9 5

ential trust. Many people would like to work for God—in an advisory capacity! With all of the religious and spiritual cynicism some have even begun to believe in themselves as a god.

When you reckon with the awesomeness of God, you are put in a position of true humility. I have come to realize that humility is not how you stack up with others, but before the God of gods—your Creator! This is what is meant by genuine humility. Once you have a sense of humility before your Creator, then you are freed up to treat everyone else with a greater respect and sensitivity.

What makes this so difficult for most is that to reckon with the awesomeness of God actually reveals your weaknesses and vulnerabilities. To be able to know and accept your weaknesses and vulnerabilities will always make you strong and free. When you don't have to cover up or deny who you really are, you save lots of energy. You also remove yourself from being a target of criticism and accusation. Since you have already revealed yourself, you can't be uncovered or embarrassed by anyone else. It's not easy to find strength in your weaknesses, because it goes against the grain of popular opinion.

The awesomeness of God puts everything in its proper perspective. But most of all, it puts you and your life in perspective by plugging you in!

Second, THE AWESOMENESS OF GOD'S CREATION! The second fundamental dimension of the Fear of the Lord is the awesomeness of God's creation. The first dimension puts you in your place of weakness before your Creator. This dimension puts you in your place of strength, due to the fact that you are the unrepeatable creation of your Creator.

In the early chapters of Genesis it's clear that men and women are created in the image of God, the Creator. There is something special about you. You are totally and completely unique. When you reckon with the Fear of the Lord, you take on the image of your Creator.

More than that, when you reckon with the Fear of the Lord, you take on your Creator as your partner. There is something psychologically and spiritually wonderful about this partnership. It's this partnership that prompted the sages of ages to say things such as "Our hearts are restless until they find their rest in God." and "Each person has a God-shaped vacuum inside that cannot be filled with anything, except God, the Creator. Nothing else fits!"

So, the Fear of the Lord is the basis for true humility—a right evaluation of yourself before God! The Fear of the Lord is the beginning of wisdom. The Fear of the Lord provides you with a most powerful LIFE AFFIRMATION:

I AM AN ORIGINAL MASTERPIECE OF GOD.
THEREFORE, I AM DESTINED
TO BE SOMEONE SPECIAL
AND TO DO SOMETHING GREAT!

This is exactly what the psalmist meant when he wrote that you are "fearfully and wonderfully made." In other words, God doesn't make junk! So, the Fear of the Lord is a fundamental piece of wisdom upon which the other six pillars stand. Do you want to be wise? Plug into your Creator!

LIFE AFFIRMATION #2—DISCERNMENT!

Without Discernment our society would be filled with all kinds of problems. Without Discernment . . .

    . . . complacency would be everywhere!
    . . . there would be no standard for right and wrong!
    . . . there would be no basis for evaluation or critical thinking!
    . . . there would be not basis for making wise choices of any kind!
    . . . most people would go along with the crowd!

*Map #2—Intellectual **RICHE$**!* 97

. . . most would not take personal responsibility for their actions!

. . . many would tend to play the role of victim!

But wait a minute! This is a precise description of our society right now!

Judge Not!

One of the most amusing habits of the human species is to quote the Bible, when it serves a self-serving purpose. The Bible is quoted so much to prove such a wide spectrum of positions on a given issue—even opposite sides of the issue. Most believe that you can find a Biblical quote that will back up your assertion no matter what it may be. This is why you can have extremists on both sides of any issue—abortion, political persuasion, racism, homosexuality—and each one use the Bible to prove their position.

At the base of this problem is the twisting, the misreading, the reading into, and the disregard for the context within which a verse is set. One of the most common misunderstandings of the Bible is "Judge not that you be not judged!" Without going into a full dissertation, it's important to understand what is meant here.

When you check out the context of this statement, it becomes very clear. There are two types of judgments—condemnation and conclusion. This is clearly saying two things. First, it is not speaking of judgment as condemnation. Naturally, no human has any right to stand in the position of condemning another human being. This is God's right and realm, not yours! Second, it is clearly speaking of judgment as conclusion. You are to make conclusion kinds of judgments about people, places and things. However, you must be careful to make your conclusion kind of judgments properly. Remember that in whatever area you make a conclusion about another person, you will draw attention to yourself in that particular area. So, before you try to take the speck out another person's eye, pull the log out of your own eye. In other words, start with yourself first! *When you don't start with yourself, you tend to overlook (deny or cover-up) your own stuff. You are then tempted to deal with everyone else's stuff and the easiest way to handle other's stuff is to judge them by way of condemnation!*

DISCERNMENT?

We are in desperate need of Discernment in our lives! Discernment is more than IQ. It has more to do with your character. It's more than gathering date and even more than experiential knowledge.

So, what is Discernment?

First, TO DISTINGUISH BETWEEN RIGHT AND WRONG! Discernment is being able to distinguish between right and wrong, good and evil, and wise and foolish. Discernment assumes that you log many hours of thought and meditation about your life. In a world where many lack a conscience, Discernment is the only dimension of wisdom that brings with it the possibility of developing one.

Conscience development is all part of growing yourself up all over again! In this dysfunctional world it is entirely possible that your conscience has experienced a stunting due to people abuse, chemical abuse, or personal abuses or neglect on your part. As is true of each of the pillars of wisdom, developing Discernment is a life-long work that will repay you with life!

Map Marker #329

First make your habits, then your habits make you!

---

*Map #2—Intellectual **RICHE$!*** 99

Second, **TO DETERMINE THE COURSE OF YOUR LIFE!**
In light of distinguishing right from wrong, Discernment can then
furnish you the power to determine the course of your life. Every
day, quite often several times a day, you find yourself at the prover-
bial fork in the road which demands your attention. You must make
a decision and live with the consequences of that decision. You must
discern which course your life will now take!

The LIFE AFFIRMATION for Discernment is . . .

**I AM ABLE TO DISTINGUISH BETWEEN RIGHT
AND WRONG, THEREFORE, I AM ABLE TO DETER-
MINE THE COURSE OF MY LIFE!**

Don't miss this dimension of wisdom! Discernment will assist
you greatly in your daily walk—for you and your loved ones!

LIFE AFFIRMATION #3—DISCIPLINE!

Solomon points out that without Discipline . . .

  . . . you will despise yourself!
  . . . you will come to poverty!
  . . . you will be dishonored!
  . . . you will lead others astray!

We live in an undisciplined society—a world that is out of control! In the
counseling room I see what I call the deadly quartet in most
everyone—fear, anger, guilt and shame. These four deadlies paralyze
people so that they can't make good progress in their lives.

Each one is an indicator that you are out of control! When you
experience *fear*, it's usually because your future is out of control. When
you get *angry to the point of festering*, it's due to your relationships or

circumstances being out of control. When you suffer from *guilt*, you can count on it; there's some unfinished business in your past that is out of control. When you are overwhelmed with *shame*, it's usually caused by the residue from your failures that resulted from your fear, anger, and guilt. Therefore, you might find yourself in a tail-spin, swirling, and very out of control!

Map Marker #92

Discipline yourself so others won't have to!

Discipline takes time and effort on your part. This is why so many are undisciplined, always looking for a short-cut, the road of least persistence! It reminds me of this MAP MARKER.

Map Marker #193

The longest distance between two points is the short-cut!

Discipline is missing in action!

Our world is so lacking in this pillar of wisdom that most parents today are intimidated away from effectively disciplining their children. In fact, in many scenes in America, if you were observed spanking your child, you could be arrested! The tide of public opinion has overwhelmingly convinced most parents that spanking in any way is a form of child abuse. Since there is so much child abuse and

Map #2—Intellectual RICHE$! 101

much of that abuse has come through the hands of angry, out of control, parents, it is easier to make a mandate against all spanking as discipline.

In my opinion, we are reaping the harvest of these faulty beliefs in our children today. We have become a society of fools and foolishness, badly in need of wisdom. Solomon frequently pointed out the fact that fools despised wisdom, especially discipline. He said "the corrections of discipline are the way to life."

Solomon illustrates discipline as an act of love. God loves mankind and therefore disciplines. A wise parent loves his child, therefore disciplines his child. He said, "the Lord disciplines those he loves as a father disciplines the son he delights in . . . . He who spares the rod hates his son, but he who loves him is careful to discipline him." (For a thorough discussion of the discipline of children, check out **The Home Improvement Kit for Effective Parenting**, listed at the back of this book.)

Solomon's words are not a blank check for beating your children or for making any kind of power-move over them. However, it is in sync with what the great writer and psychiatrist, Scott Peck, has to say regarding what discipline is all about. He says, "discipline is love translated into action." What a powerful statement and what a great truth that is missing in action in our world!

Map Marker #206

Character does reach its best until it is disciplined!

DISCIPLINE?

So, what is Discipline? Remember that Discipline is an expression of an interpersonal relationship of love. Discipline seeks the reformation and restoration of people. Education is the goal. With this in mind, let's look at the two basic dimensions of Discipline.

First, CORRECTION! As in each of the seven pillars of wisdom there are two critical parts to Discipline. The first is correction. As you make your way along your personal journey you can live a life of denial and cover-up—a life of defending your actions and excusing yourself. Or, you can live a life of learning and openness—a life of growing and developing yourself to be more productive. You can whitewash yourself or you can work on yourself. You can excuse yourself from personal responsibility or you can embrace the opportunity to be responsible for yourself and your actions. *The role of correction within Discipline is the touchstone that makes the difference!*

Be careful not to fall into the trap of seeing Discipline as correction only. This a common parental trap in the discipline of their children. It's a simple thing to correct your child with a word, such as "No! Don't do that!" To stop doing something or to only correct an action or behavior is just half of the equation in understanding what Discipline truly is. Correction is definitely important, but without the second dimension, correction may end up being a punishment. This is where most parents fail in their attempts at Discipline. Discipline is not just correction. There is so much more!

Second, INSTRUCTION! The second half of Discipline is instruction. Instruction is the most difficult and the most productive part of Discipline. Correction is usually quick and takes very little thought. Instruction requires more time and some careful thought.

Years ago I set out to discipline my son for trashing the garage. He was very young, but I sent him out to clean up the destruction he and his friend had created and to sweep up the garage. When I went out to check on him, I discovered that he lacked a plan on how to approach the job and therefore, was not accomplishing much to-

*Map #2—Intellectual **RICHE$!***   103

ward a positive conclusion. This is when I realized that I had to jump into this situation and do some work (instruction). When it came to sweeping the garage, it was difficult to determine whether his method was sweeping the dirt in or sweeping it out! So, I entered into a short workshop on how to sweep the garage. We finally finished the project and I learned the most important lesson in the process. Discipline requires more than correction. It must include instruction—and instruction takes lots of time and patience!

The LIFE AFFIRMATION for Discipline is . . .

I WANT TO LOVE MY SELF SO MUCH THEREFORE, I GLADLY PRACTICE DISCIPLINE ON MY SELF AND PROMOTE DISCIPLINE FROM GOD AND FROM OTHERS!

LIFE AFFIRMATION #4—KNOWLEDGE!

Map Marker #422

What you don't know won't hurt you—
until you find out
someone is getting paid for knowing
what you don't!

Solomon progresses to Knowledge as the fourth pillar of wisdom. He quickly points out how foolish it is to reject Knowledge . . .

. . . How long will mockers delight in mockery and fools hate knowledge?

. . . Wise men store up knowledge, but the mouth of a fool invites ruin.

. . . Whoever loves discipline loves knowledge, but he who hates correction is stupid.

. . . Stay away from a foolish man, for you will not find knowledge on his lips.

. . . It is not good to have zeal without knowledge, nor to be hasty and miss the way.

Without Knowledge you are stupid, foolish and will miss out on life! Without Knowledge your life becomes out of focus and blurry!

Map Marker #182

Knowledge is like a snapshot. It can be enlarged,
but if it gets out of focus, everything becomes a blur!

It's through Knowledge that you develop your belief system that sets the course of your life! Solomon encourages acquiring Knowledge . . .

. . . For wisdom will enter your heart, and knowledge will be pleasant to your soul.

. . . Choose my instruction instead of silver, knowledge rather than choice gold.

. . . Every prudent man acts out of knowledge, but a fool exposes his folly.

. . . The lips of the wise spread knowledge; not so the hearts of fools.

. . . The discerning heart seeks knowledge, but the mouth of a fool feeds on folly.

*Map #2—Intellectual **RICHE$!*** 105

. . . The heart of the discerning acquires knowledge; the ears of the wise seek it out.

. . . Gold there is and rubies in abundance, but lips that speak knowledge are a rare jewel.

. . . Apply your heart to instruction and your ears to words of knowledge.

. . . A wise man has great power, and a man of knowledge increases strength.

KNOWLEDGE?

True Knowledge is not just learned or memorized; it is lived and experienced! Knowledge is to know something or someone experientially—to really know it! This is the use of the word in the Bible when it speaks of a man knowing a woman. It is to know her as completely as possible—to know her intimately—sexually!

Map Marker #117

Knowledge without doing
is like plowing without sowing.

You are to take on Knowledge in such a way so that you know something intimately—experientially. Knowledge requires your participation. This kind of Knowledge is not concerned about whether or not it will be on the final exam in a given course of study, but embracing Knowledge as it applies to your ultimate final exam in the course of life! This reminds me of the following MAP MARKER . . .

Map Marker #82

Some students drink at the fountain of knowledge.
Others just gargle!

There is something exceptionally attractive about a heart for
Knowledge that demonstrates a teachable spirit. When you position
yourself as a learner, you set yourself up to get through any crisis that
presents itself—even the self-afflicted variety!

So, what is Knowledge?

First, TO GATHER DATA! When defining what Knowledge
is, most would jump to the conclusion that it is the gathering and
storing of information. Everyone has had the experience of having
to memorize lists of names and all sorts of details for exams at school.
The better memory you have the better you'll do in the school system. Since I memorize things easily, I was able to do very well in
school. Whether or not I actually learned something was not measured by many of those dreadful exams.

Gathering information is not the end of what Knowledge is all
about, but it is a necessary foundation to build upon. Therefore, to
obtain Knowledge you must take in more and more information. I
like the sign on a high school bulletin board in Dallas: "Free every
Monday through Friday—knowledge. Bring your own containers!"
You have to go for it!

Second, TO GRASP IT FOR YOURSELF! The second dimension gives Knowledge its fullness. It's not enough to just gather
the data, you must grasp it for yourself. Possess it! To experience
what you know is true Knowledge!

Map #2—Intellectual RICHE$!   107

Map Marker #207

A little knowledge properly applied
is more important than a tremendous number
of facts accumulated and not utilized.

Map Marker #146

The wise carry their knowledge
as they do their watches
—not for display but for their own use!

The LIFE AFFIRMATION for Knowledge is . . .

**I AM ABLE TO LEARN ALL KINDS OF THINGS,
BUT I DON'T WANT TO KNOW ONLY TO LEARN;
I WANT TO KNOW IN ORDER TO REALLY LIVE!**

Map Marker #163

Knowledge is power—only when it is turned on!

LIFE AFFIRMATION #5—WISE BEHAVIOR!

God created you with five senses plus horse and common. It's
unfortunate that common sense isn't more common! Recently

observed trends in the corporate and mass marketplaces have a basic cry. "We want someone to help us make sense out of this or that!" We are all in need of having someone to help us make sense out of our lives. Why? There is a desperate wisdom drought in our world— a lack of horse and common sense!

Map Marker #41

Horse sense means stable thinking!

Map Marker #61

Common sense is the sixth sense,
given to us by the Creator
to keep the other five from making fools
of themselves—and us!

Wise Behavior maybe be best defined as wise dealing. It's doing that which is right, appropriate, and with great beauty and balance! Wise Behavior has no hint of being reactionary in your behavior. There is a quiet, controlled confidence that has no need to be reactive, but proactive. Wise Behavior is the essence of a truly successful lifestyle. It knows nothing of the superficial or shallow success that is so showy in the marketplace today. Wise Behavior is wholesome, relevant, and attractive!

Map #2—Intellectual RICHE$! 109

WISE BEHAVIOR?

So, what is Wise Behavior?

First, TO COMPREHEND IN ORDER TO USE GOOD COMMON SENSE! Society is always taken by surprise by any new example of common sense. I am continually amazed at how effective I am when I deliver to an audience simple, common sense. Over the years I've come to realize that my best stuff is truth simply expressed in terms of common, down-to-earth sense!

Map Marker #72

Common sense is the knack
of seeing things as they are,
and doing things as they ought to be done.

In a real sense, Wise Behavior requires that you develop a personal philosophy of life. Your philosophy of life is developed as you formulate a world view. Why are you here, what do you own and what are you to do with who you are and what you own? It's concluding how life works best.

Map Marker #123

Philosophy is nothing but common sense
in a dress suit!

Second, TO CONFORM YOUR LIFE TO THE CHARAC-TER OF GOD!   There is an imprint within every human being—an image indelibly imprinted on your psyche. Some might call it the "ideal self", but I call it the mark of your Creator upon your soul. When you contemplate what the perfect character would be, you can do no better than to imagine the character of God.

This personal character of God is at the core understanding of the addict who has learned to relate to his Higher Power. He turns his will and life over to God—not a god who has no character, but to God, who possesses the most wholesome, the most relevant, the most beautiful, the most balanced, the best image of character ever imagined!

Wise Behavior becomes yours as you seek to conform yourself to this image of God. In an earlier chapter I presented this exercise as discovering your unique purpose in life. Your purpose is written on an inner label, placed in your soul by your Creator. Follow this mark! Conform yourself to this image of the character of God and how you are to reflect it in and through you and you will develop this highly desired pillar of wisdom—Wise Behavior! And, you will experience a most full and completely satisfying personal success! For many years I have defined success in the following way . . .

Map Marker #97

Success is being & doing
all that you were created to be & to do!

When you conform your life to the character of God, you will be successful! When you don't, you may look successful, but you're really not—it's too shallow and sadly superficial!

Map #2—Intellectual __RICHE$__*!*   111

The LIFE AFFIRMATION for Wise Behavior is . . .

I AM A REPRESENTATIVE OF GOD, THEREFORE I MUST CONFORM MY LIFE TO GODLY ATTITUDES AND GODLY ACTIONS!

LIFE AFFIRMATION #6—PRUDENCE!

The sixth pillar of wisdom that Solomon presents is Prudence. The absence of prudence is to be gullible and to be trapped. Without Prudence it's easy to jump to conclusions, make foolish decisions, trust everyone, trust everything that is in writing, and find yourself caught in the many traps that are set for the unaware.

TRAPS SET BY PEOPLE!

Gullibility is taking everyone and everything at face value without expending energy toward getting to the truth. It's an inability to see through people—to see what's really happening! Therefore, you are an easy target for those who set traps to get you to do whatever they want you to do. These are traps set by people for other unsuspecting and unaware people!

People also trap you by pulling you into feeling dependent upon them. They want you to need them in the worst way. People or relational addiction could easily be the most common of all addictions that plague our lives!

TRAPS SET BY YOU!

The most common trap that you set for yourself is the 'time trap.' The tension is between 'then' and 'now.' 'Then' has two possibilities that will trap you—the future trap and the past trap!

The future trap is living on 'Someday I'll' . . .

There is an Island fantasy
A "Someday I'll," we'll never see

When recession stops, inflation ceases
Our mortgage is paid, our pay increases
That someday I'll where problems end
Where every piece of mail is from a friend
Where the children are sweet and already grown
Where we all retire at forty-one
Playing backgammon in the island sun
Most unhappy people look to tomorrow
To erase this day's hardship and sorrow
They put happiness on "lay away"
And struggle through a blue today
But happiness cannot be sought
It can't be earned, it can't be bought
Life's most important revelation
Is that the journey means more than the destination
Happiness is where you are right now
Pushing a pencil or pushing a plow
Going to school or standing in line
Watching and waiting, or tasting the wine
If you live in the past you become senile
If you live in the future your on Someday I'll
The fear of results is procrastination
The joy of today is a celebration
You can save, you can slave, trudging mile after mile
But you'll never set foot on your Someday I'll
When you've paid all your dues and put in your time
Out of nowhere comes another Mt. Everest to climb
From this day forward make it your vow
Take Someday I'll and make it yours Now!

My good friends, Leonard and Vicki Crowfoot, recently shared with me "At our age, SOMEDAY is not just another day in the week!"

*Map #2—Intellectual **RICHE$**!*   113

At any age you can't afford to make the theme of your life SOME-DAY. SOMEDAY may never become a reality to you! SOMEDAY is a trap!

The other trap is the past trap. When you live in the past, you exist in a musty archaeological dig, full of massive ruins that cannot be changed. With archaeology, you have two options. You can live there or you can learn from having been there. The real trap is living there. Living in the past is like having a huge rear-view mirror, larger than your wind-shield! This situation makes it very difficult to make any effective, forward progress in life. You must look out of your car door window to move ahead. And if you only look at the rear-view mirror, you will most certainly crash into something else and suffer damage!

So, what is Prudence?

First, THE ABILITY TO SEE THE TRAPS THAT CONCEAL THE TRUTH FROM YOU! This is not an innate ability, but it is acquired and vital to your personal success. Unfortunately, the ability to see through the traps normally comes through the experience of being trapped or tripped up by the many traps that are set. A mentor can help, but still, more is learned through experience than any other way!

Second, THE ABILITY TO SEEK THE TRUTH THAT IS REALLY THERE WITHIN THE TRAP! Truth is always present in a good trap. Otherwise, there is little effectiveness in the trap. Without a measure of truth there is little to lure you into the trap. Cheese carefully placed in the mouse-trap! Bait deceptively luring the fish to the hook! Even in rat poison, you have about 96% nutrition and only 4% that will kill you!

Prudence is the ability to see the trap, seek the truth in the trap and sort it out! The Hebrew word for Prudence was used of stripping away the bark of a tree and getting to the basic trunk of the tree. It's the ability to get to the heart of the matter in every situation you face. It's getting to the clarity of the bottomline of most of life's issues. Prudence, then, gives you a new sense of freedom as you make your way through life.

The LIFE AFFIRMATION for Prudence is . . .

**I AM ABLE TO SEE THROUGH THE TRAPS OF LIFE
AND TO LIVE MY LIFE ON THE BOTTOMLINE,
THEREFORE I AM ABLE TO LIVE MY LIFE FREELY!**

LIFE AFFIRMATION #7—PLANNING!

Without Planning your life is directionless and a life without direction tends to lack one of the most life-giving ingredients of all—hope! Without a purposeful Planning it's too easy to float—to take up space. I'm convinced that *without a healthy sense of Planning you tend to promote the principle of death and dying rather the principle of life and living.*

Map Marker #138

A life without a plan is like traveling to
an unknown destination without a map!

You can readily see why you purpose is so vital to this pillar of wisdom as well. Your purpose determines and drives your plan!

So, what is Planning?

First, TO CONSIDER THE FUTURE OF YOUR LIFE!
Without a doubt, the best way to plan your life wisely is to consider the future of your life with the end in view. What do you want the end results to be? What will people say about your life, when it's all

*Map #2—Intellectual **RICHE$**!*   **115**

over? What will be said in the eulogy? Consider the future of your life! What do you want to be said at the end?

Second, TO CAST THE FUTURE OF YOUR LIFE! In a large measure you can determine what will be said at the end of your life and you can start today. You can cast the future of your life starting today!

On several occasions I have spoken on "It's Your Funeral!". I walk through how I would prepare to conduct the funeral or memorial service of anyone. Then, with this outline, I encourage people to fill in the blanks. What do you want to be said? What is the picture you want to paint? What is most interesting is, you are painting the picture right now. How are you doing?

The LIFE AFFIRMATION of Planning is . . .

I HAVE A DREAM PLACED IN MY HEART BY GOD— A MISSION I MUST FULFILL, THEREFORE I'M DETERMINED TO DISCOVER THIS DREAM AND MAKE IT HAPPEN—NO MATTER THE CONSEQUENCES!

III. THE INTELLECTUAL RICHES PICKUP . . .

Map Marker #29

You can commit yourself
to something over an over again,
but if you don't talk your mind
into going along with it,
your commitment will fizzle out!

The Brains of the Outfit

You can commit yourself to picking up any of the riches, but there's a built-in fizzle in your commitment unless your mind is constantly in control. Your mind is the control-center of everything that's you! It's the "brains of your outfit!"

If you are going to pick up your intellectual riches, you must take control of your mind—the control-center! And it's up to you to take control of your own mind, and then start being, feeling and behaving in the ways you choose rather than be directed by the herd!

Meditation is a psychological tranquilizer! (Check out your workbook for practical suggestions on how to meditate most effectively.) Remember, it brings the most genuine prosperity you could ever possess—inner prosperity. Peace of mind, wisdom, control of annoying habits, relief from destructive stress, the ability to view your problems through a wider perspective, a greater sensitivity to yourself and your relationships, patience and endurance during the various trials of life. Whatever your stress problem, you'll find meditation can be a mental adrenaline that will boost you into the "controls" of you, your relationships, and your future! Now, you are ready to pick up your INTELLECTUAL RICHES—all seven of them!

Chapter 6

Map #3—Career *RICHES!*

I. THE CAREER RICHES PROBLEM . . .

There once was an owner of a prominent 'head-hunting' organization who had pitched thousands of people, selling them on the various career opportunities he represented. He was known for his persuasive ability, a giant in the public relations business. One day while walking down the street he was tragically hit by a bus and he died. His soul arrived up in heaven where he was met at the Pearly Gates by St. Peter himself.

"Welcome to Heaven," said St. Peter. "Before you get settled in though it seems we have a problem. You see, strangely enough, we've never once had anyone in the public relations field make it this far and we're not really sure what to do with you." "No problem, just let me in."

Well, I'd like to, but I have higher orders. What we're going to do is let you have a day in Hell and a day in Heaven and then you can choose whichever one you want to spend an eternity."

"Actually, I think I've made up my mind . . . I'd prefer to stay in Heaven."

"Sorry, but rules are rules . . . " And with that St. Peter put him in an elevator and it went straight down to hell.

The doors opened and he found himself stepping out onto the putting green of a beautiful golf course. In the distance was a country club and standing in front of him were all his old friends fellow PR guys that he had worked with over the years.

They were all dressed in tuxedos, beautiful women on their arms, and they were all cheering for him. They ran up and slapped him on his back and they talked about old times. They played an excellent round of golf and at night went to the country club where he enjoyed an excellent steak and lobster dinner. The Devil, who was actually a really nice guy, came over and offered him a Cuban cigar. Then he and all his pals loaded into a limo and went to the most amazing restaurant and bar he had ever experienced.

He was having such a good time that before he knew it, it was time to leave. Everybody shook his hand and waved goodbye as he got on the elevator. The elevator went up-up-up and opened back up at the Pearly Gates and St. Peter was waiting for him. "Now it's time to spend a day in heaven."

So he spent the next 24 hours lounging around on clouds and playing the harp and singing. He had a great time and before he knew it his 24 hours were up and St. Peter came and got him. "So, you've spent a day in hell and you've spent a day in heaven. Now you must choose you're eternity."

He paused for a second and then replied, "Well, I never thought I'd say this, I mean, Heaven has been really great and all, but I think I had a better time in Hell."

So St. Peter escorted him to the elevator and again he went down-down-down back to Hell. When the doors of the elevator opened he found himself standing in a desolate wasteland covered in garbage and filth. He saw his friends were dressed in rags and were picking

Map #3—Career RICHE$! 119

up the garbage and putting it in sacks. The Devil appeared to him, ugly and frightening, came up to him and put his arm around him.

"I don't understand," the PR man stammered, "Yesterday I was here and there was a golf course and a country club and we ate lobster and we danced and had a great time. Now all there is nothing but a wasteland of garbage and all my friends look sad and miserable."

The Devil looked at him and smiled. "That's because yesterday you were a prospect. But today, you're a client."

Careers are filled with promises! Money! Good working conditions! Benefits! Retirement! However, you are more likely to experience just the opposite. Many find that the corporate ladder they have been climbing and climbing over the years either doesn't go all the way to the top as they were promised or that their ladder has been leaning against the wrong building all along!

Beware of depending upon your chosen career, whatever it may be, to be your care-taker or your guardian angel for life. The tendency is to be so dependent that you become emotionally crippled. You tend to become so reliant on your career—employer, corporation, governmental benefits—that you lose your God-given sense of self-reliance and self-confidence. With this perspective your career depletes your energy—your very life—for the sake of the company!

Your career riches have been accumulating for someone else!

As is true with all of the other riches, you must become proactive and pick up your own career riches! Let's take a look at the basic principles for building your career riches.

II. THE CAREER RICHES PRINCIPLES . . .

Most of my speaking is in the corporate marketplace. In this arena I have had to opportunity to meet with some of the most successful people in the world! Most, not all, have discovered something that becomes their secret of success. Each has found a game plan for success that includes four dynamic ingredients—personal, people, professional and permanent success!

I have identified a core principle within each of these ingredients. I call them "power-sticks"—four sticks of dynamite that empower you toward living your life most successfully. Or, to put it another way, these power-sticks are able to empower you being and doing all that you were created to be and to do!

PERSONAL SUCCESS

The first ingredient is a strategy for personal success! You must develop a game plan for personal success. All success begins with the person—you! This is the process of becoming. Without a sense of success in your personness there will always be an inner time-bomb threatening to sabotage all external successes in your life.

The Power of Incarnation!

To avoid creating this kind of time-bomb or detonating one that has already been set, you must focus on your inner, personal success. Here I want to introduce you to the first power-stick—**the power of incarnation!**

The power of incarnation has to do with taking on your inner purpose of life and using your best efforts to make it happen. Incarnation means to take on an identity—fleshing out what's inside! The power of incarnation requires that you seek to clarify what your inner purpose is.

The power of incarnation reveals the genuine power of individuality. We live in a world that minimizes the individual's power and influence. You have to fight this atmosphere of diminishment on every hand. The world of *Atlas Shrugged* is upon us! It's a world of disempowerment at most every level! Experts disempower! The gov-

*Map #3—Career **RICHE$!***   **121**

ernment disempowers! Religious leaders disempower! Educators disempower! Parents disempower!

The power of incarnation empowers! You and your efforts do make a mark upon your world. That is a fact! The real question is what kind of mark is it or will it be? Check out this poem, THE POWER OF ONE . . .

One song can spark a moment,
One flower can wake the dream.
One tree can start a forest,
One bird can herald spring.
One smile begins a friendship,
One handclasp lifts a soul.
One star can guide a ship at sea,
One word can frame the goal.
One vote can change a nation,
One sunbeam lights a room.
One candle wipes out darkness,
One laugh will conquer gloom.
One step must start each journey,
One word must start each prayer.
One hope will raise our spirits,
One touch can show you care.
One voice can speak with wisdom,
One heart can know what's true.
One life can make the difference,
You see it's up to YOU!

Don't ever forget how
very important YOU are.

To Know Your Self Is To Love Your Self

The power of incarnation requires that you really get to know your self. As you identify and clarify your inner purpose in life (Remember, this is an ongoing process—a work in progress!) you learn about who you are. I learn more and more about myself when I think about things, when I ask questions of others, when I answer other's questions, when I read, and when I interact with life as it is and people as they are. You know the old saying, "To know me is to love me!" Take this to heart! Get to know your self and you will begin to love your self! Self-knowledge is self-love!

Map Marker #130

Love your neighbor as yourself.
If you don't love yourself,
your neighbor's in a heap of trouble!

Before even considering how to cultivate love relationships with other people, you must first cultivate a love relationship with YOU! Self-love is not to be confused with selfishness. Selfishness is the very opposite of self-love! Selfishness is a form of greed which produces an insatiability—a perpetual sense of never being able to reach satisfaction. It's a bottomless pit! This is the same as a narcissist profile—a person who is totally into himself, restless, impulsive, and filled with envy of all others who seem to have more . . . driven by a great fear of not getting enough, of missing something, of being deprived of something. Although the selfish person is into himself, he doesn't like himself, but lives with an intense dislike of himself. Therefore, his or her entire life is expending energy overcompensating for this basic lack of

Map #3—Career <u>RICHE$</u>!   123

self-love. If you are into selfishness, you are fundamentally incapable of loving yourself or anyone else! So, self-love is a necessary ingredient for building healthy and growing relationships.

Probably the most common misunderstanding in the world of relationships is the fact that intimacy begins with your relationship with yourself and not with a relationship with another human being. Most people are looking for someone else to bring the joy of intimacy into their lives. It just doesn't happen that way! Intimacy begins inside you! This is why you may have heard the popular statement: BE THE ONE BEFORE YOU FIND THE ONE!

I conduct intensive workshops on intimacy with a variety of couples. The most critical issue that must be understood is that you bring your own baggage into every relational encounter and you are responsible for your own behavior—your own stuff! You see, it's easy to speak the truth about others, but very difficult to tell the truth about yourself. It's impossible to produce a healthy and happy relationship with two unhealthy and unhappy people!

An amazing dynamic occurs when you are honest about yourself. Every time you are brutally honest about yourself and avoid any form of denial or cover-up, you become like a mirror to others. You mirror to others their dishonesty and their denial. This presents an interesting decision point for everyone you touch. Each person has to decide whether to be honest, telling the truth about himself, or keep playing the game of denial and cover-up.

This kind of experience happens daily with the addict who makes the decision to stop the denial and fess up about his problem. This open, honest confession and determination to clean up his life presents a major problem for everyone in his world—his spouse, his kids, his addict buddies, his colleagues, etc. Everyone has become used to relating to him in a certain way. Now, his honesty forces everyone to change, too. Or, instead of changing there is also the option of running away.

So, self-knowledge brings about self-love, which, in turn, sets you up to experience personal success! With the foundation for building your personal success you are now ready to work on the second level of your game plan for success.

Choices—To Choose Or Not To Choose?

Personal success means facing reality. Probably the toughest reality you will ever face is that you are the product of your choices. Your power is in your choices! If you find yourself stuck in a destructive situation, you don't have to stay there. You must make some choices to get out of where you are! You may or may not have chosen loneliness, but you have the power to choose not to be lonely. You didn't choose for you loved one to die, but you, and only you, have the power to choose to go on with your life. You may not have consciously chosen the disease that plagues you, but you have the power to choose to handle it. You may not have desired that divorce, but you do have the choice of recovery from the relational wounds. You may feel that you are a victim of anorexia or overweight, of alcohol or drugs, of gambling or smoking, of sick relationships or no relationships, but you have the power of life and living or death and dying within your power to choose!

Unsuccessful people tend to make few choices for themselves. They allow other to make decisions for them, coasting along unwilling to make the tough decisions for them. But to make no choice is a choice—to lose!

Choosing is one of the four most significant acts that make you a healthy human. Wise choices enable you to grow up. Foolish choices, others' choices, and no choices force you only to grow old.

PEOPLE SUCCESS

The second ingredient is a strategy for people success! You must develop your game plan for people success. First, you must focus on

Map #3—Career __RICHE$__!   125

your person-ability and then, your people-ability. This is the process of relating. Without a sense of success with the people in your life you will leave an interminable trail of relational wreckage behind you. And this wreckage will weigh you down in the present, so that you will live out a predictable course of relational disaster after disaster.

The Power of Interdependence!

In order to avoid certain, predictable disaster you must focus on building your people success. This is where the second power-stick comes into play—**the power of interdependence!**

Interdependence has two enemies. These enemies are actually the two extremes that make up the word. They are independence and dependence. People success requires that you possess both. One without the other spells certain disappointment and relational failure.

Independence is standing on your own two feet. It's being self-contained. Only an independent person has something to offer in a relationship. Dependence is supporting another and being supported by another. It's a mutuality. Dependence is only healthy when it's built upon independence.

Interdependence is a balancing act between independence and dependence. This balance is the power that drives true people success! Interdependence undergirds all people success—from your experience of teamwork in the marketplace to your most intimate relationship. Nothing illustrates this more vividly than the typical flock of geese!

Geese Know Better Than Humans!

Next Fall when you see geese heading south for the winter, flying along in a V formation, you might be interested in knowing what science has discovered about why they fly that way. It has been learned that as each bird flaps its wings, it creates an uplift for the bird immediately following. By flying in a V formation, the whole flock adds at least 71 percent greater flying range than if each bird flew on its own.

Whenever a goose falls out of formation, it suddenly feels the drag and resistance of trying to go it alone, and quickly gets back into formation to take advantage of the lifting power of the bird immediately in front. When the lead goose gets tired, he rotates back in the wing and another goose flies at the point. The geese honk from behind to encourage those up front to keep up their speed. Finally, when a goose gets sick, or is wounded by a shot and falls out, two geese fall out of formation and follow him down to help and protect him. They stay with him until he is either able to fly, or until he is dead, and then they launch out on their own or with another formation to catch up with their original group.

Do you fly in a V formation? At work? At home? In your personal life?

Who Cares?

Fractured and fragmented families and friendships are overwhelming proof of how tough it is to win in relationships. When your relationships aren't working, it's because a primary ingredient is missing.

Caring is the key success factor for people success. This is the second most significant act that can make you a healthy human. Caring and being cared for are channels for energy flow. No quality life can be developed without it.

Map Marker #71

Life cannot grow in a vacuum!

Map #3—Career <u>*RICHE$!*</u>   127

When you are plugged into relationships in a healthy way, three factors can emerge from these relationships. These three factors, necessary for healthy relationships, are: appreciation, accountability, and action. These are indicators of who really cares—who gives a rip whether you live or die.

Appreciation

An old hunter took his new retriever out early one morning to test him out. The old man shot his first bird, and the dog immediately darted after it. When the dog reached the water, he walked on top of the water, picked up the dead bird, returned on top of the water, and brought the bird back to his master. The old hunter rubbed his eyes in disbelief but decided it really didn't happen. He set himself up to shoot again. Again he shot a bird, and again the dog retrieved the bird by walking on top of the water. The hunter was amazed at his dog's behavior.

The old hunter wanted to show off his wonderful hunting dog to his best friend. So he invited him to go out hunting early the next morning. His friend got the first shot and hit a bird. The dog walked on top of the water, picked up the dead bird, returned on top of the water, and brought the bird back to his master. The old hunter said, "Do you notice anything different about my new dog?" His friend nonchalantly replied, "No, looks like just another bird dog to me."

They sat up for a shot at their next victim. This time the old hunter shot the bird out of the sky. Again, his remarkable dog walked on top of the water and retrieved the bird. The old hunter asked again, "Are you sure you don't see anything different about my new dog?" His friend thought a moment and said, "Why, yes, that dog can't swim!"

Appreciation is the first critical factor in a relationship. You don't need people who always tell you what is wrong with you. You need people in your life who will appreciate what is right with you. You must be in a relationship where you are appreciated. You need positive strokes, someone who genuinely cares about you. Everyone needs those warm fuzzies!

When you are appreciated, you know that someone cares. You are empowered by that caring!

Accountability

A middle-aged woman made her way into an apartment building to the twelfth floor. As she arrived at her intended destination, she rang the doorbell impatiently. The door opened mysteriously, and she was welcomed by the smell of incense and smoke. She entered and was greeted by a slightly dressed young girl who announced her presence with the sounding of a huge gong. With this the young girl said, "Do you wish to see the all-knowing, all-powerful, the wonderful one, Maharishi Naru?"

"Yeah," the woman said. "Tell Sheldon his mother is here!"

Accountability is the second critical factor in a relationship. There's nothing like the loving accountability of a mother. Nothing like it, except for the loving accountability of true friends plugged into caring relationships.

Accountability keeps you true to who you want to be and how you truly want to live. Accountability means that someone cares enough to hold me to you to your commitments. When you make commitments, you need to be plugged into people who will help you be responsible enough to keep them. It's not being responsible for you, but responsible to you.

Accountability also means caring enough to confront you when you're off-track. It's constructive criticism bathed in genuine appreciation. Destructive confrontation is a criticism with no intention of supporting the suggested change. Constructive confrontation is a

*Map #3—Career **RICHE$!***   **129**

criticism in which the one who confronts is willing to personally pitch in and support you in whatever way they can.

Map Marker #94

An open rebuke is better than love in secret!

Action

A rabbit being chased by a dog through the countryside was observed by a crowd enjoying a family picnic. They cheered for the rabbit as he swiftly hopped from side to side, masterfully eluding his attacker. Then the rabbit pulled away from the dog a great distance, looked at the crowd and said, "I appreciate your encouragement, but shoot the dog!"

Action is the third critical factor in a relationship. It is the final ingredient necessary for healthy, caring relationships. You need people in your life who are willing not just to say, "Hey, I'm your friend; you can count on me," but to act those words out and shoot the dog. This is the action factor within caring relationships.

Caring is the second of the most significant acts that make you a healthy human. You need this caring and everyone around you needs the same caring from you.

PROFESSIONAL SUCCESS

The third ingredient is a strategy for professional success! You must develop your game plan for professional success. First, it was your person-ability then, your people-ability and now your profession-ability. This is the process of achieving.

Achieving requires personal responsibility. Be careful of either being overly responsible or irresponsible. Over-responsible is acting out as a control freak! You are not responsible FOR anyone else; you're only responsible TO others. However, you are responsible FOR yourself!

Irresponsibility is an extreme of a different color. Irresponsibility breeds excessive blaming and excusing away of all personal responsibility. This has become an epidemic in our world! Don't get caught up in it!

The Power of Impact!

In order to avoid wasting your life you must grapple with what kind of difference you are making with your life. To make a positive difference you must take personal responsibility for your life, because no one else will! This is where the third power-stick comes into play—**the power of impact!**

There are three depressing thoughts that must be shared at this juncture, so that you can use the power of impact for yourself.

First, no one is as excited as you are about what you are doing! Check it out! This is a simple truth, but profound in its impact upon us. We all want people to be like us, go along with us, and to share our excitement on whatever it is that we're excited about! But count on it! No one is as excited as you are about what you're doing! So, don't expect anyone to be!

Second, there is no group meeting right now in which they are taking about how to make your life successful! Now, there may be a group sitting around talking about you right now, but I guarantee you that your success is not the primary subject of their discussion. Don't allow yourself to slip into the trap of thinking that someone or a group of someone's out there will someday bail you out of your circumstances into a whole new, set of wonderfulness! It's just not going to happen like that!

Third, if anything good is going to happen in your life, you must make it happen! This may sound a little 'heady' to you, but it's absolutely true! *You must make it happen!* You may have difficulty

Map #3—Career __RICHE$!__   **131**

with this approach to life, especially if you believe in a Higher Power or a relationship with God. But consider this story . . .

A farmer took a desolate piece of land behind his farmhouse, exhausted himself in cultivating several plants and created a most impressive garden. After the various vegetables began to show their goods, the farmer called his priest to come and see this beautiful sight!

When the priest arrived to view the garden, he couldn't stop talking about what kind of beauty God had created. "Look at this corn! God sure makes great corn, doesn't He?" "Wow, look at these peas, tomatoes, and the cabbage! God sure does make incredible vegetables!" Well, the farmer is beginning to feel a little frustration with the priest's reaction. I mean, he had spent lots of time in this pile of dirt and really sweat in order to produce this fabulous garden!

The priest continued his praise of God and His creation and the farmer continued to become more and more frustrated with not getting any credit for what he had accomplished. Finally, the farmer had taken about as much as he could take, when he said, "I wish you could have seen this garden, when God was doing it by Himself!"

This is the point! God does incredible, miraculous work! But He works in partnership with you! In other words, if anything good is going to happen in your life, you must make it happen!

And, if you are going to be a make-it-happen kind of person, you must seek to cultivate creativity. Do you remember what I said earlier in this book, "It's not what happens to you, but how you handle what happens to you that counts!" When you are creative, you are effectively handling whatever may happen to you!

Creating?

Creating is the third of the most significant acts that make you a healthy human. It's the responsibility to create, to make something meaningful out of your life. It's the weaving of your abilities (no matter how small) and your energies (no matter how weak) into a life fabric that has significance. Instead of coasting through life watching what happens, you must make life happen!

One of the great stories of all time is about a store-keeper who was enveloped by two aggressive stores—one on each side. One store put up a sign that said, "Lowest Prices Ever!" On the other side of his store was the sign that read, "Best Bargains On Earth!" These two stores on either side were promising more than he could ever deliver! After sleeping on it, he woke up and went directly into his store to create a new sign. In big, bold letters his sign said, "ENTRANCE!" Now, that is handling what happens to you! That is creating!

PERMANENT SUCCESS

The fourth ingredient is a strategy for permanent success! You must develop your game plan for permanent success. First, it was your person-ability then, your people-ability, your profession-ability, and finally, your profit-ability through permanent success.

Notice how we have progressed to this point. In order to grow up from childhood into adulthood, everyone must pass through the basic processes of life . . .

The Process of Becoming through which you find personal success.

The Process of Relating through which you find people success.

The Process of Achieving through which you find professional success.

It's important that you also note that nobody is able to move through these three processes of life perfectly, therefore it is necessary to either repeat these processes continually or to grow yourself up all over again. In other words, there is another life process that everyone must pass through. I call this the process of regenerating!

The process of regenerating is a recovery process that you must repeatedly walk through until you get it! There is absolutely nothing

Map #3—Career RICHE$!   133

wrong with this process. It's all a part of the human condition and human-conditioning!

I have a basic theory in life. You tend to learn so much better during times of trials and trouble. I hate that theory, but I know it's fundamentally true!

Think of it like this. There are three scenarios that bring clarity to the principle. First, you are speeding down the freeway and suddenly come upon a highway patrolman at the side of the road. He doesn't stop you, but your foot immediately reacts by pulling off the accelerator and moves straight to the brake. Did you learn anything in this incident? Maybe you learned to be more careful or to watch more diligently for law enforcement.

Second, you are speeding down the freeway and suddenly come upon a highway patrolman who pulls you over to give a ticket. The ticket costs a little over $340. Did you learn anything in this incident? Maybe you learned that it can really cost you, when you speed or when you ignore the possibility that you could get caught for it.

Third, you are speeding down the freeway and suddenly loose control so that you crash into other vehicles, ending up in the ditch. You are now lying in the Intensive Care Unit. You're going to live, but the pain is excruciating! There is no doubt in my mind that it is this painful situation that teaches you most effectively!

Map Marker #31

The quality of learning lessons correlates directly with the pain associated with the lesson!

This is why I call this level of success permanent. It's at this level, in the midst of or as the result of your pain, that you learn the best, the most, and you tend to learn things forever, if not longer! It's indelible! It's permanent!

The Power of Improvement!

The process of regenerating requires the fourth power-stick— **the power of improvement!** Embracing the power of improvement brings sanity in the midst of the most insane, troublesome times of your life. You learn that every disappointment, every failure and every conflict are obstacles with opportunities embedded inside them. You must dig them out for yourself!

Map Marker #116

Problems are plows that prepare the way
for planting significant seeds of success!

The power of improvement is actually the power to get through it—whatever it may be—to go through it and to grow through it! The power of improvement gives you a most healthy perspective on your life, especially when things go wrong. Check out this prayer . . .

Lord, are you trying to tell me something?
For FAILURE does not mean I'm a failure;
It does mean I have not yet succeeded.
FAILURE does not mean I have accomplished nothing;
It does mean I have learned something.
FAILURE does not mean I have been a fool;
It does mean I had enough faith to experiment.
FAILURE does not mean I've been disgraced;

Map #3—Career __RICHE$!__   1 3 5

It does mean I dared to try.

FAILURE does not mean I don't have it;

It does mean I have to do something in a different way.

FAILURE does not mean that I am inferior;

It does mean that I am not perfect.

FAILURE does not mean that I have wasted my life;

It does mean that I have an excuse to start over.

FAILURE does not mean that I should give up;

It does mean that I must try harder.

FAILURE does not mean that I will never make it;

It does mean that I need more patience.

FAILURE does not mean you have abandoned me;

It does mean you must have a better idea. Amen.

Constructing?

Constructing is the fourth of the most significant acts that make you a healthy human. Remember, it's not what happens, but how you handle what happens to you that really counts! Constructing contains the idea of building through every circumstance, not only problems.

There are many frustrating circumstances that demand the principle of constructing. In my early days I set out to go from point A to point H. Now that, in itself, is not a problem. The problem occurred when I wanted to go straight to H without experiencing B, C, D, E, F and G. You see, when you want to go to H, the tendency is to go to H right now! And, to settle on B through G seems to be a waste of time or a distraction. No matter how beneficial stopping at B through G may be, it isn't H. And you want H right now!

The principle of constructing gives you a wider perspective on your dilemma. In life, you must go to H by way of B through G. You can go straight to H, but you won't be able to settle there for long and enjoy the benefits of being there. You aren't ready for H until you have been to B through G!

Therefore, when your goals are set high on a certain position, a job, an opportunity, an amount of money, a skill level or whatever, most of the time it is necessary to take lesser steps to get to where you want to be at some point in the future. This reminds me of one of Murphy's Laws that I placed into a MAP MARKER.

Map Marker #307

When you set out to do something, you always
find other things that must be done first!

View every step along your journey as a step that you can build upon. Take each step and use it to make progress toward your ultimate life goals. Viewing life in this manner will eliminate wasted energy and time.

Again, this is why it's so vital to articulate your life's purpose, because this purpose is the definition and clarification of your ultimate life goals. With your purpose in mind you are better able to take each and every step that presents itself to you in your journey toward a total success—that which is personal, people, professional, and permanent!

Map Marker #288

Even if you're on the right track,
when you stop you're likely to get run over!

Map #3—Career RICHE$!   **137**

PURPOSE IS A CALLING!

I mentioned earlier that your purpose is an inner label placed by your Creator. It is a fundamental calling upon your life. Calling is another term for your vocation. You have a job and then you have a vocation—a life calling! When you are called, you must answer your calling. So, take it seriously and follow it until you die!

PURPOSE IS CONSECUTIVE!

Your purpose is consecutive. It's progressive! It progressively builds on past pain and problems. Those who have experienced the devastation of paralysis tend to have a calling to assist others who experience the same thing. This is true of most every tragedy or difficulty—chemical addiction, disease, financial disaster, marital and family stresses and all kinds of disabilities. Your purpose will most likely be molded by the events of your past—usually the more difficult events mold the best!

Map Marker #129

Don't ever learn to spell cat. Once you do that, they keep on giving you harder words!

PURPOSE IS A CONTINUUM!

Your purpose is on a continuum. Your purpose is the Ultimate Goal that drives the rest of your goals. You set every other goal according to your purpose—your Ultimate Goal! This means that you drop each goal that is outside of your Ultimate Goal. You must view each goal as a stepping stone toward your Ultimate Goal and give it your full, undivided attention and energy!

Without practicing your purpose you'll discover that there are no career riches, only jobs!

Map Marker #135

The place of your calling is the place
where your deep gladness
and the world's deep hunger meet.
It's the thing you need most to do
and the world needs most to have done!

III. THE CAREER RICHES PICKUP . . .

In a very real sense, picking up your career riches requires:
that you retool your life's strategies . . .

    strategy for personal success
    strategy for people success
    strategy for professional success
    strategy for permanent success

that you re-evaluate yourself in the four primary life processes . . .

    process of becoming
    process of relating
    process of achieving
    process of regenerating

and that you re-learn life's lessons . . .

    learn to choose
    learn to care
    learn to create
    learn to construct!

Chapter 7

Map #4——Health *RICHE$!*

I. THE HEALTH RICHES PROBLEM . . .

Poor Johnson had spent his life making wrong decisions. If he bet on a horse, it would lose; if he chose one elevator rather than another, it was the one he chose that stalled between flowers; the line he picked before the bank teller's cage never moved; the lane he chose in traffic crawled; the day he picked for a picnic there was a cloudburst; and so it went, day after day, year after year.

Then, once, it became necessary for Johnson to travel to some city a thousand miles away and do it quickly. A plane was the only possible conveyance that would get him there in time, and it turned out that only one company supplied only one flight that would do. His heart bounded. There was no choice to make; and if he made no choice, surely he could come to no grief.

He took the plane.

Imagine his horror when, midway in the flight, the plane's engines caught fire and it became obvious the plane would crash in moments.

Johnson broke into fervent prayer to his favorite saint, Saint Francis. He pleaded, "I have never in my life made the right choice. Why this should be, I don't know, but I have borne my cross and have not complained. On this occasion, however, I did not make a choice; this was the only plane I could take and I had to take it. Why, then, am I being punished?"

He had no sooner finished when a giant hand swooped down out of the clouds and somehow snatched him from the plane. There he was, miraculously suspended two miles above the earth's surface, while the plane spiraled downward far below.

A heavenly voice came down from the clouds. "My son, I can save you, if you have in truth called upon me."

"Yes, I called on you," cried Johnson. "I called on you, Saint Francis."

"Ah," said the heavenly voice, "Saint Francis Xavier or Saint Francis of Assisi. Which?"

This is precisely the dilemma that we all face in the world of health! It's a world of conflicting and confusing information—and much of it is fatal! *Good news:* Honey is good for you! *Bad news:* 40 percent   of all honey on the market today may be fatal to children under a year old. *Good news:* sodium nitrite, used in hot dogs, bacon, lunch meat, and so on, prevents botulism! *Bad news:* sodium nitrite can cause cancer! *Good news:* Saccharin, an artificial sweetener, can be used as a substitute for harmful sugar. *Bad news:* Saccharin can also cause cancer! You're doomed if you do and doomed if you don't! You can't seem to win!

II. THE HEALTH RICHES PRINCIPLES . . .

Health is measured in a variety of ways. Unfortunately, the most common theme around health and the medical community is treating the painful symptoms rather than promoting a healthy lifestyle. Specialization in treating these symptoms requires that you have to

Map #4—Health <u>RICHE$</u>!   **141**

learn how to diagnose yourself before you know which specialist to call. I've heard it said that the physical condition of a man can best be judged from what he takes two of at a time—stairs or pills.

Whatever you think of health riches, there is one thing that always rings true with respect to your health: *Anybody who thinks money is everything has never been sick!* Your health is one of the most valuable riches you'll ever know!

Map Marker #106

The human body, with proper care, will last a lifetime!

A lot of people lose their health trying to become wealthy, and then lose their wealth trying to get back their health. True health riches boils down to two simple dynamics—subsistence and self-control!

The Dynamic of Subsistence!

The first is the dynamic of subsistence—eating and exercising.

Eating right. There's more disagreement here than you'll face in most any subject, other than religion. But when you think of it, it only makes sense that there is such diversity. Since people are so diverse, it only stands to good reason that there is no THE WAY to eat that is universally healthy for everyone on the planet.

What works for some doesn't work for others! Take the very negative publicity that smoking and drinking receive. Yet you can interview elderly people everywhere who have enjoyed a smoke or a drink every day of their lives and lived to be in their 80's, 90's or over 100!

This is why diets vary so much! One approach may not work for everyone!

Having said this, there are a few universal truths that you can successfully embrace for yourself and to your health. Most everyone agrees with a low fat, high fiber diet, avoiding chemicals, and consuming as much live, natural foods as possible.

You must study it for yourself, learn, and listen to your body for a clear confirmation of what works best for you. You are the best expert on you and how you feel! So, become an expert on you!

Exercising regularly. What sort of exercise and how much is also very controversial. There is a myriad of systems being marketed from every corner of the planet. Some encourage the use of machines, some urge free-weights, others sell contemporary contraptions and still others suggest no weights of all.

Again, it is universally agreed since most live and work in a sedentary environment that it is important to do some sort of real or artificial WORK on a regular basis. When I lift weights, jog, walk or play basketball, I look at it as doing some WORK. I spend so much time in front of a book, a computer or people seeking counsel that I just don't get a chance to do much physical WORK in my daily work. Therefore, I plan to do this WORK, at least, five days per week and more, if at all possible.

Not only is this supposed to be good for my heart and body, it makes me feel really good. I enjoy the feeling of doing the WORK and having WORKED! And, I find a greater benefit in doing this WORK than enhancing my physical well-being. I find that I am a more disciplined person in my life—emotionally, spiritually and intellectually, when I discipline myself physically!

The Dynamic of Self-Control!

Easing stress. Many people suffer poor health, not because of what they eat, but from what is eating them. I already rehearsed the

*Map #4—Health **RICHE$**!*   143

destructiveness of the stress mess in the previous chapter. I watched my mother die of cancer, but I later realized that the true cause of her death was not cancer. She was ravaged by stress! In her case, stress disguised itself in the cloak of cancer. Stress uses a variety of disguises, but the results are all the same—death and destruction!

Everyone handles stress differently, therefore you need to constantly evaluate how you can ease the stresses in your life, with your loved ones, and in the pursuit of your livelihood. If you're honest with yourself about your stress-load, you can determine how you can specifically pace yourself to avoid it's deadliness.

Empowering your self. All of the dimensions above—eating right, exercising regularly, and easing your stress are minor compared to *empowering your self*. The greatest health threat to your success and your riches may be what is commonly called 'being stuck'— stuck in the cycle of destruction! There is no greater drain on the corporate marketplace, on communities, on friendships, on families, and on individuals than being stuck.

STUCK: No One Is Exempt!

stuck, *v.* to be brought to a standstill, blocked, baffled, halted, obstructed; *n.* a state of difficulty or hesitation. Stuck shows itself in a lot of different forms: alcohol, drugs, workaholism, food, disease, suicide, death, molestation, divorce, relationships, rebellion, anger, guilt, phobias, handicaps, loneliness.

When you examine them, some forms of stuck—such as alcohol and drug abuse—seem worse and have a greater stigma. Others— such as death, deadly disease, and physical handicaps—seem to be victimizing attacks against humanity. Less obvious are the more common forms of stuck—such as compulsive work, hidden spouse or child abuse, divorce for convenience, impulsive affairs, disguised loneliness, occasional or chain smoking. These situations are rarely marked as desperate problems. But they are! And you can get just as stuck in them!

We are all stuck! That's right—all of us, and no exceptions. It doesn't matter where you look, whether you turn to your doctors, neighbors, ministers, friends, counselors, all of us (at least at one time or another) are stuck!

Strange, isn't it, that our enlightened society knows more and can do more than at any other time in world history, yet stuck is all around. We have more self-help information and programs than ever before in virtually every known problem area. Yet stuck is not only around, it keeps growing. Think about it. Eating disorders and drug abuse are on the increase. Alcoholism negatively affects one-third of all American families. We may know more about life, but we still don't know how to live life!

If you remain stuck, you go nowhere, you do little that promotes life, and you view life from a narrow perspective. Being stuck is like hanging by a skyhook. The hook controls you, and you can't enjoy stability or make progress. Life demands growth (stability and progress), but stuck stunts human growth. Stuck drains your life and drives you toward a certain self-destruction.

THE BAD NEWS: We are all stuck!

THE GOOD NEWS: We can all start over!

If for some reason a person told you that you are a horse, it's best just to ignore it. If a second person told you that you are a horse, it should be cause for concern. You might want to check your hoofs. But if three people call you a horse, then maybe it's time to saddle up!

If the symptoms and indicators of being stuck start to mount up, then it is time to saddle up and start over. Let's take a look at the basic symptoms and indicators that point to being stuck in the cycle of destruction?

Map #4—Health RICHE$!   145

It's Time To Saddle Up
. . . When the Undesirable Increases

Stuck problems are indicated by compulsive patterns that increase in frequency and produce undesirable consequences! Life should be a process of doing more and more of what produces desired results. It should not be a repetition of doing things that produce undesirable results. As you mature, your behaviors that produce the undesirable should be eliminated and replaced with behaviors that result in the desirable.

Compulsive eating and drinking are good examples. When a heavy person gets heavier because of compulsive eating, when that person continues to eat uncontrollably and gain more weight, and when that person hates more and more to look in the mirror with the addition of every new pound, that person is stuck—caught in a cycle of destruction! Crash diets that reduce weight for two months are indicators of the same problem when the weight is replaced with even more fat in four months. The diet that produces temporary results is undesirable. It only prevents the desired state of normal weight from occurring!

Many alcoholics, when asked about the effects of drinking, will relate pleasurable feelings of warmth, security, and euphoria. They fail to mention the broken marriage, disturbed children, morning-after sickness, or the pleading, yelling, and screaming that often accompany a drinking binge. Even if it has been twenty years since the drinking has provided pleasurable memories, alcoholics will hold on to the belief that alcohol continues to produce desirable results.

As undesirable results and repeated tragedies mount up, people rationalize that life is tough and full of sorrow. Well, it may be, but so often the tragedies can be avoided with a change in behavior due to the recovery process. When undesirable results increase, rather than accepting that it is "just life," the person is better off asking, "What am I doing to contribute to this?" Accepting responsibility

for correcting the problem comes from admitting that a specific behavior not only produces undesirable results, but also increases the
frequency of the undesirable.

. . . When You Feel a Need to Control

*Stuck problems are indicated by repeated attempts at control that end
in relapse!* When something is not a problem, you don't have to control it. You don't have to control the urge to eat carrots. Why? It's
not a problem! People who have a problem with gambling attempt
to control the gambling. Men who have a problem with extramarital affairs attempt to control the urge to merge with women other
than their wives. Alcoholics attempt to control their drinking, and
workaholics attempt to control their time away from home. The
problem areas are obvious to objective observers. Areas that need
control are problem areas and they indicate that a person is stuck in
the cycle!

. . . When You Are Filled with Anguish

*Stuck problems are indicated by repeated frustration and short-term re-
sults from attempts to control the behavior!* Anguish lives where hope is
dying. It's caused by a complete lack of direction in resolving the problems that increase in intensity. Because repeated attempts to control
the problem produce only short-term results, anguish sets in. It flour-
ishes in the midst of conflicting advice from family and friends.

Anguish is pain combined with anxiety. The person feeling anguish fears the future because in addition to intensification of the
problem, the consequences of the problem cause pain. The harder
the efforts at controlling the problem, the greater the anxiety and
pain. Living in anguish is like having a dark cloud hovering above.
It grows into the belief that to be alive is to be miserable.

Everyone has problems. But when normal problems are combined with anguish over more severe problems, the results can be
devastating. In an effort to cope, people often drink heavily or seek

Map #4—Health __RICHE$!__ **147**

relief through a drug of some sort. This compounds the problem and feeds the anguish already in existence. Problem upon problem piles up to make misery more miserable. A simple problem causes frustration, but repeated problems produce anguish beyond frustration and life without hope!

. . . When You Experience Withdrawal

Stuck problems are indicated by the immediate urge to repeat compulsive behavior that is stopped! When a person in the cycle of destruction stops a compulsive behavior, that person has an immediate urge to repeat the behavior. This urge is called withdrawal. Withdrawal often dashes the hopes of stuck people 'who are attempting to resolve problems on their own. When will-power is mustered up, the person makes the decision to change and finally stops the behavior. Withdrawal drives the person into starting the destructive behavior all over again!

Smoking, drinking, abusing drugs, and eating have some chemical withdrawal involved that makes the withdrawal problem more complicated. But with some problems, the emotional attachment is stronger than chemical addiction. Someone caught up in an extramarital affair knows the agony of withdrawal when attempting to stop the unhealthy relationship. Emotional withdrawal can be so intense that it makes the person physically ill, as if there were a chemical withdrawal also. Whether it's the need to stop having a relationship or to stop making trips to the refrigerator, withdrawal and the urge to repeat the negative act indicate that the cycle has its grip on the person.

. . . When There Are Repeated Disasters

Stuck problems are indicated by repeated tragedies that result in still more tragedies or disasters! It's clear that a person is in the cycle of destruction when tragedy results in still more tragedies or disasters. Repeated tragedies can't be passed off as mere bad luck. When a family is riddled with personal problems—such as financial crises, teen-age drug abuse, divorce, and legal problems—it's no accident or quirk of fate. The cycle begins by entrapping first one family member and then trapping the entire family. When the entire family becomes a disaster, one or all are stuck in the cycle!

... When You Feel the Brick Walls of Isolation

Stuck problems are indicated by walls that are thrown up to keep others out! The opposite of being hooked on life is going through life in isolation. Loneliness is not the normal condition for human beings. It's abnormal for people to increase their isolation through working too much or changing residences or always having to be the leader.

Alienation from others makes people feel as if everyone else is different, that no one understands or could understand. Alienated people fear relationships, and they fear pain that has resulted from destructive relationships in the past. Since growth and life can't happen in a vacuum, alienation can only bring about more tragedy and misery.

People who experience alienation are often surrounded by people. They appear to be active and involved. But a closer look reveals that there is no communication going on. There is a sharing of information without any personal sharing of one another. Being surrounded by people isn't a protector from alienation. Sometimes it feeds into it!

For a lot of people, it's time to "saddle up" and get on the road to starting over. When the evidence piles up and points to a serious problem that intensifies day after day or year after year, it's time to do something about the problem.

But moving out of the cycle or that comfortable rut takes courage. It takes courage to be willing to cut from your life that which is preventing the desirable from happening. It seems that it would be a simple choice to move out of a cycle of destruction and start over into a healthy life and lifestyle. But it's a complicated system of un-

Map #4—Health RICHE$!   **149**

healthy dependencies that locks a person in, that destroys the willingness to cut off the problem!

III. THE HEALTH RICHES PICKUP . . .

Three Steps to Starting Over!

Human nature goes against the need to start over. It's human nature to hide problems, to cover them up and not talk about them. It's natural to take the path of least resistance, to do what is easiest at the time. Getting unstuck is never easy. It goes against the natural reactions that have compounded the problem. In other words, it takes real courage to start over—to truly empower your self. It takes real courage to pick up your health riches!

STEP ONE: Confession—Courage to Open Up to Another!

This first step is an old concept. People really don't like to talk about it. It's been reclassified through time and labeled as old-fashioned and unnecessary. But it's vital to the healing process. Covering up and hiding your problems will make you sick! As you are able to reveal more and more about your areas of stuckness, the layers of isolation and alienation can be shattered.

Map Marker #90

You are as sick as your secrets!

Self-revelation and confession is a gradual process, like peeling an onion layer by layer. It must be done carefully. Too much too soon only leads to more problems. When years of troubles have been bottled up and concealed and then carelessly spewed out to a friend, it's embarrassing to both. This only increases the alienation. When the walls of concealment are dropped quickly, they are usually stronger when reconstructed.

Confession is really nothing more than agreeing with someone that a problem exists. It's not revealing every indiscretion that has ever happened with all of the details. When denial stops, confession can begin. When done properly, confession can be a tremendous relief as openness starts to develop between two people. As the sharing gradually increases, a new freedom is experienced by the one who has suffered alone for too long.

Problems with sex are perhaps the most frequently hidden problems of all, especially problems from the past that constantly creep up on a person and cause self-doubt and self-discrimination. The frequency with which people cover up and stay stuck in this area is of epidemic proportions. People frequently find that simple revelation can heal the past.

After I spoke one evening, a man came up to discuss a problem he had been struggling to handle. I had known him for a couple of years. He had an attractive wife and a brand-new baby. He told me he was stuck with a problem that he couldn't resolve.

He was very reluctant to say anything to me, but he was so miserable that he had to talk with someone. It was a sexual problem, not of action but of thought. He reconfirmed his love for his wife to me, then he shared the difficulty. Before he was married he had had sexual relationships with many women over a period of years. Every time he made love with his wife he found himself obsessed with thoughts and images of one particular woman from his past. The more he tried to stop, the more he obsessed and the more frustrated he became.

Map #4—Health RICHE$!   151

As I discussed his problem with him a little further I reassured him that he had just begun to take care of the problem. His courage to open up about it at the risk of destroying his image with others would lead him to the relief he had been seeking. Sure enough, he reported to me a few weeks later that he finally experienced freedom. He was free of these old images! Shattering the isolation with open confession is the first step back to health and starting over.

Too many people are stuck because of their unwillingness to open up and confess their problems. Small, even insignificant problems can grow in severity because they are concealed. Pride prevents people from admitting their own humanness and ability to stumble or to fail. Humility, instead of pride, allows a person to be free of the problems of the past through the process of admitting and confessing irresponsibilities. The biggest irresponsibility of all is the unwillingness to confess the little ones. Confession unlocks the freedom and the relief that are available to anyone who is stuck. But confession is just the first step.

STEP TWO: Communication—Courage to Relate Within a Group!

Communication within a supportive community is the second step. It must be an ongoing process in order to pick up all of your health riches. It's more than just a one-time confession of irresponsibility. It's also a discovery of the real person beneath the façade. Communication within a supportive community involves facing reality and expressing emotions that evolve from that reality. It's the ability to listen and to accept others as they express different feelings about the same reality.

A supportive community can come in many different forms and sizes. It might be called a self-help group, a growth group, a recovery group, or a therapy group. Whatever the name, or whether it has three or thirty people, the supportive community is made up of individuals who are willing to admit that they are all strugglers together in this world and that the struggling is made easier when openness and honest communication form the base of relationships. And in these relationships there is accountability to one another.

The supportive community provides a place where communication can be practiced and improved. It's a place where you can not only confess your irresponsibility but also learn to communicate support and encouragement for others. It's a place to discover that others have experienced many of the same problems and have survived, and to hear their insight from having overcome the difficulties. Communication with a supportive community is vital for starting over from any level of stuckness. To be able to open up and reveal problems, even when it's difficult and painful, is a survival skill that must be developed. Without this skill, this ability to communicate with a few trusted friends, picking up your health riches can only be a temporary experience!

STEP THREE: Commitment—Courage to Do Whatever It Takes!

Commitment to do whatever it takes is the third step in starting over. It involves the courage to cut out of life whatever is preventing the achievements that are desired and deserved. Commitment means to stop trying to convince the world that the problem can be handled alone. Doing whatever it takes involves working with others toward recovery rather than attempting to solve the problem alone. Commitment to do whatever it takes is the ability to say, "I'm stuck, and I'm ready to do whatever it takes to get rid of the problem." This kind of commitment is made of courage!

Commitment to the convenient will never do. Courageous commitment to do whatever it takes is a necessity for picking up your health riches. Often a lifetime is spent attempting to untie and untangle problems that need to be severed. Whatever is standing in

Map #4—Health RICHE$!   153

between your hope of empowering your self and the reality of doing something about it must be cut off as soon as possible, no matter how painful!

Picking up your health riches is more important to you than it is to anyone else. No one can pick them up for you; you must have the courage to do it yourself!

Robert A. Raines in his book, **Creative Brooding** (New York: Macmillan, Inc., 1977), relates a story about the courage of a logger in the backwoods of Oregon. In order to transport logs from the of the mountain down to the river below, the loggers constructed large wooden chutes. They would cut down a tree, strip off the limbs, then place the huge trunk in the chute and slide it down to the river. By the time the logs reached the river, they were traveling very fast. They would hit the water, then float down the river to the mill.

The loggers used the wooden chutes to save time and effort in getting from the top of the mountain to the bottom. Rather than walk to the bottom, they would place an ax in the chute and ride down on the handle. It saved time and it was exciting and lots of fun.

One day a logger slid down the chute on his ax handle and attempted to get out of the chute when he reached the bottom. But when he stood up, he slipped. His foot became lodged in between two of the large wooden planks that made up the chute. It was wedged in tight. As he struggled frantically to pull it out, he heard the yell, indicating a huge tree trunk was being sent down, from on top of the mountain. In desperation he struggled harder, trying to get out of his boot or free the foot. But there he stood, his foot caught in the planks, the huge trunk speeding toward him, and all he had was his ax. He was stuck, and the only way out took courage from within. That man had the courage to cut from his life the only thing that stood between him and certain death. He axed off his foot and jumped free in time to save his life. Most would have died trying to untie a boot that would not come free.

Attempting to untie and untangle what must be cut has caused many deaths or other tragedies. It has kept people in the cycle of destruction and destroyed their ability to live freely. But there comes a time when a person must say, "I have eaten enough!" or "I have drunk enough!" or whatever! When that point is reached, confession, communication, and commitment can move you away from the cycle of destruction—*from* stuck to starting over!

Starting Over Starts Today!

Picking up your health riches requires that you empower yourself by emancipating yourself from being stuck and start over. Starting over can occur at any point in your life—whenever you discover that you're stuck! Starting over can be the beginning of a new life more beautiful and more meaningful than ever imagined. One person's problems can be the source of inspiration for others who experience similar problems and work to overcome those problems. It all begins with admitting that a problem exists and confessing that problem openly and honestly to another person. Followed by honest communication and the commitment to do whatever it takes, these three steps begin the adventure of starting over.

Whenever you become aware that you are stuck, start over . . .
By confessing!
By communicating!
By committing to do whatever it takes!

Map Marker #318

The relative values of wealth and health depend on which you have left!

Chapter 8

Map #5—Emotional *RICHE$!*

I. THE EMOTIONAL RICHES PROBLEM . . .

Your emotional riches are very difficult to quantify. Their invisibility and fluidity make it nearly impossible to easily get a handle on them so that you can manage them effectively. Your emotions may be conscious, sub-conscious, or unconscious, but all of them are for real! They may be negative, positive or neutral, but they will have their effect upon your life, loved ones and livelihood. They will affect your riches—mostly through your attitude!

So instead of grappling with an analysis of your emotions, I want to give you some handles on how to cultivate your attitude in a most effective way. Your attitude can make all of the difference in the world with respect to how you handle all of the rest of your riches that you want—relational, intellectual, career, health, financial, and spiritual. Possessing the right attitude is one of the most important ingredients to build your net worth! When your attitude is set, your actions follow accordingly.

Filling Up the Hole in Your Soul

At the core of your attitude is your soul. Your soul is either full of life or it's on empty. Focus on the soul has increased over the last 10 years. More and more are realizing the desperate need for filling up the hole in the soul! When your soul is full, you know what it means to be satisfied. Healthy emotions can only be grown in the seedbed of a satisfied soul.

Everyone is looking for satisfaction—total satisfaction! Some call it joy or happiness. Some call it peace. And others call it fulfillment. However, no matter how much people want satisfaction, it has become extremely illusive!

Most insist on searching for satisfaction in all of the wrong places. In fact, there is a common tendency among mankind to seek satisfaction or happiness from *other people, places, or things*! People can only contribute or take away from your satisfaction or happiness; they can't make you happy. Places are nice and maybe even beautiful or exotic, but places can't make you happy or bring you satisfaction. Things can be wonderful—especially expensive things, but things can't make you happy either. People, places and things can bring satisfaction for a temporary period of time. Note that this kind of satisfaction is good and temporary, but it's not the best and it's not long-lasting!

Map Marker #82

Almost anything can be bought at a reduced price except lasting satisfaction!

Pseudo-Satisfaction

Pseudo-satisfaction is easy and most common in this world. In my many years of personal study and through counseling several thou-

Map #5—Emotional <u>*RICHE$!*</u> **157**

sand people I have come to understand what pseudo-satisfaction is made of and how it is attained. Most of the time people seem to slip into pseudo-satisfaction by default—no other options were known. But no matter how people arrive at it, pseudo-satisfaction is just that—pseudo—false!

There seem to be four modes of arriving at the pseudo-satisfaction destination and each one builds upon the other. Let's briefly take a look at each mode and gain some understanding at each level, so that you know what to avoid in your search.

Map Marker #70

Satisfaction is the best kind of internal revenue!

Alienation Mode

We live in a world of pseudo-satisfaction, primarily because mankind has become unplugged—uncentered—displaced and detached! There's a certain sense of alienation in the air—a sense of the impersonal! You will find it difficult, if not impossible to live within the many impersonal systems for one very simple reason—your own personness! Personness can't fit within the impersonal. It's like a fish attempting to live out of water, or a train maneuvering through a field without a set of tracks. It just doesn't fit!

To many, man is a collection of molecules, a stimulus-response machine, or a highly developed animal. But when he views himself as just molecules, a machine, or an animal, he becomes extremely frustrated and dissatisfaction sets in on the gut-level.

The primary alienation seems to be with your own soul. I think it has to do with being unaware of your relationship with your Creator. This, to me, is what I mean by being unplugged—a self-alienation.

The interesting thing is that this initial alienation from your Creator triggers further dissatisfaction in your relationships with others. The very relationships that should supply the most to you become the most disappointing—sucking the very life out of you!

Attachment Mode

The alienation mode moves naturally into the attachment mode. Once you have become unplugged from your Creator and alienated from your self, you must seek to attach to something or someone outside yourself. This move requires others or other things to bring satisfaction into your life. Now, these people, places or things must come through for you or you build up an inner rage about those people, places and things. You take on a rage about life . . . an inner dissatisfaction that seems to perpetuate itself.

Antagonism Mode

Alienation leads to an attachment mode which produces antagonism. This level of inner dissatisfaction is a deep antagonism that continues to fester and boil inside your soul. You can identify this result by watching life's daily results in the world around you. This is the source of what you read in your daily newspapers—abuse, rape, homicides, suicides, murder-suicides, angry mobs marching for their rights or standing for their causes, freeway shootings, the soaring divorce rate, the digging up dirt on any public figure, the besmirching of another's character in the press, abandonment, angry lawsuits, the delight seen in watching another powerful person fall, the intense hate for those who have wealth, and the killing sprees by elementary school kids!

Absurdity Mode

Alienation . . . attachment . . . antagonism! When you are caught on this roller-coaster ride, you can easily give up on life. At least,

Map #5—Emotional RICHE$!   159

you may find that you have lost your ability to hope any more. It's what I call the absurdity mode. Nothing makes much sense any longer. Most everything is meaningless—going through the motions. This is a low-grade depression—an embalming process that produces a zombie-like, herd mentality of survival! This makes it impossible to reach out beyond yourself to make a difference in another person's life, because you are too concerned about your own survival to care for someone else. And, with this approach to life, you can only reach a point of pseudo-satisfaction. With this approach to life, your life is fixed in an automatic default that makes true satisfaction illusive.

II. THE EMOTIONAL RICHES PRINCIPLES . . .

THINKING + DOING = FEELING

What you think affects your feelings! "As a man thinks in his heart, so is he." This has become a proven fact in the arena of medicine. Your blood pressure can be elevated by what you're thinking. Your cholesterol levels can soar out of sight through stressful thinking!

Not only does negative thinking cause negative results, but opposite is also true. A few years ago my son joined the high school cross-country team. The Corona Del Mar High School cross-country program under Coach Bill Sumner enjoyed a great legacy of winning teams—regionally and statewide, although the school was one of the smallest in the State of California. He was a freshman and excelled in his first year to the point of making the varsity team.

Toward the end of the season the team was scheduled to run what is known as the 2nd most difficult course in the Nation. This particular course has three major hills that can break the best of runners on a normal day. As this event approached we were in a heat wave and the smog was intense. On the night before the event, Timothy was gripped with fear about finishing this tough course in a respectable time and expressed it to me. As I thought about what he was thinking, I attempted to encourage him. I told him that I had found that I would rather run hills than just a boring flatland and that when I approached a hill, I attacked it and did quite well. I suggested that maybe it was in the Timmons' genes to run hills well. He bought it!

The next day he ran one of the best races of the day! He had a confidence that was incredible throughout the race. I watched him on those hills. He was bursting up those horrible hills and breaking the spirits of those he passed. When he came across the finish line, he looked so pale and almost unconscious. In fact, he was! It took the paramedics an hour to get him back on his feet. (The paramedics were busy that day with runners suffering from heat exhaustion all morning!) He didn't remember the last mile of the three mile race! The power of what you think is amazing! What you think directly affects how you feel—about yourself, about your relationships, about your profession, about your life!

What you do affects your feelings! Think of it this way. You think, feel, and do. Depression is when you do not do, but only think and feel. It's an endless cycle of think-feel, think-feel, and think-feel. You may first think things are bad and when you check your feelings, you feel bad. The worse you feel, the more you think about how bad it is. It's think-feel! That's depression and it's bad! The only way you can break this cycle so that you change your feelings of depression is to do something—*anything*! What you do affects your feelings!

Again, this is both positive and negative. When you do bad things, you will feel it. When you do good things, you feel good. This is a case of clear cause and effect. What you do affects your feelings!

Map #5—Emotional RICHE$!   161

INSTANT RETURN ON YOUR EMOTIONAL INVESTMENT

Here is an incredible phenomenon! I call it an instant return on your emotional investment. When you do something toward another person, you actually share in it. And when you think something toward another person, you share in it, too. When you show mercy and compassion toward someone, you receive mercy and compassion at that very moment! Right then and there! When you forgive, you experience the wonderful relief and warmth of forgiveness in the act of forgiving! When you love someone, you are experiencing that very same love at that very moment! When you pray for someone in need, you receive that same experience expression of love back into your own soul at that very moment!

This isn't the same as karma where you send out something good and you get it back. This is totally different and much more powerful! You see, the problem with karma is that you must wait to catch the return on your investment—whether it's good or bad. (Now, waiting is not a problem when you have sent out some bad karma, but waiting for the good to come back is not as easy.)

The dynamic of instant return on your emotional investment is not only instant; it's wonderful! This brings some of the words of Jesus into focus, when He said, "Love your neighbor as yourself." . . . "Blessed are the merciful, for they will receive mercy." . . . "If you forgive, you will be forgiven." It is instant and it is wonderful—for others and for you!

A HEALTHY, WEALTHY ATTITUDE . . .

As I mentioned earlier, personal satisfaction is quite costly! And the primary cost to you is paying the price to develop the disciplines necessary to produce a healthy and wealthy attitude.

In my personal search for inner satisfaction I have discovered 8 life disciplines that have the power to transform your life from the inside out! When I encounter any other set of disciplines that offer such a benefit, these 8 stand firm a cut above all of the rest in their power for change and their practical effectiveness.

The fundamental reason for this great power and effectiveness is that each of the disciplines works from the inside out. The first 4 deal with your inner self. The second 4 have to do with your inner self as you relate to others. And, when you stand each quartet of disciplines next to one another, they powerfully and practically inter-relate with one another.

The disciplines that I have discovered come from an ancient speech given by one of the most powerful and influential people who ever lived! In a book, *A Few Buttons Missing*, Gerald Fisher, an eminent psychiatrist, views this speech as the summation of the most complete statement of psychological health ever given in one speech or one writing (article, chapter, or book). In fact, he states that there is no better articulation of the essential principles of mental health than is summarized in these basic attitudes!

Let's briefly examine each discipline and I'll explain where I found them later . . .

#1 REAFFIRM YOUR POVERTY

To reaffirm your poverty means to have a right evaluation of yourself before self, God, and others. All of life begins right at this point. Possessing a right evaluation of yourself before self, God, and others is true humility—the exact opposite of the blindness of pride.

Pride is one of the seven deadly sins; it's universal among humans and it's devastating! Pride always seeks to be exalted, to be first and to be praised. (Don't misunderstand! There is a good sense that some people identify as pride as in self-confidence or self-satisfaction, but I believe it's helpful to call it just that—self-confidence or self-satisfaction.) Pride blinds you to the point that you don't see

Map #5—Emotional __RICHE$!__   **163**

your self for who you are becoming, you position others in a crippled, weakened condition, and you begin to think that you may be God—the center of the universe!

Pride is not always blatant. It's an insidious cancer that skews your thinking, distances you from enjoying your relationships, and sets you up for a fall in whatever you do.

Map Marker #81

Some people get credit for being cheerful, when they are really just proud of their teeth!

Reaffirming your poverty is the recognition of your spiritual bankruptcy. It's coming to grips with your humanity! I have brought upon myself the most devastation when I have violated this attitude. I used to believe I could jump over buildings (or anything in my way) in a single bound. I knew I could break through brick walls, no matter how thick. There was nothing much that I could not do or overcome!

But I want to confess to you that with this prideful attitude. I have enjoyed many successes, but I have endured many failures. A better way to say it is that on many occasions in my life I have failed miserably! Just to be able to recognize those failures is a freeing experience. The tendency is to reframe every one of those horrible experiences, blame someone or something else for what went wrong, and rid myself from those marks against me.

What I've learned is that it is through the pain of the miserable failures that I've grown the most. In the midst of that pain I have learned vital truths about me, God, and the others in my life.

To reaffirm your poverty is to stand at the threshold of the best of your life. This is precisely where those who must overcome their

addictions have to begin. Without a doubt the most effective movement over the last several decades has been AA, Alcoholics Anonymous. This originated as a recovery movement for those who were
struggling with the abuse of alcohol and its devastation upon their
lives. It has grown to include those who are struggling with nearly
every kind of problem imaginable—drugging, gambling, eating, sex,
shopping, relationships, etc. The real beauty of this movement is
that in order to find healing—to find life—you must recognize your
own inadequacies. You must come to grips with your humanity. You
must enjoy true humility—a right evaluation of your self, God, and
others. You must reaffirm your poverty!

I am convinced that those who are struggling along in their recovery groups may be the most blessed people of all, because they
have been forced by the gravity of their problem to face themselves,
God and others more honestly. I am also convinced that everyone
struggles with a problem that he must face head on in order to find
true sanity and freedom in life. The only place to start is through
this vital discipline of reaffirming your poverty. The Twelve Steps
begin right here:

1. We admitted that we were powerless over our problem—that
   our lives had become unmanageable.
2. Came to believe that a Power greater than ourselves could
   restore us to sanity.
3. Made a decision to turn our will and our lives over to the
   care and direction of God as we understood Him.
4. Made a searching and fearless moral inventory of ourselves.
5. Admitted to God, to ourselves, and to another human being
   the exact nature of our wrongs.
6. Were entirely ready to have God remove all these defects of
   character.
7. Humbly asked Him to remove our shortcomings.

Map #5—Emotional __RICHE$!__   **165**

8. Made a list of all persons we had harmed, and became willing to make amends to them all.
9. Made direct amends to such people wherever possible, except when to do so would injure them or others.
10. Continued to take personal inventory and when we were wrong promptly admitted it.
11. Sought through prayer and meditation to improve our conscious contact with God as we understood Him, praying only for knowledge of His will for us and the power to carry that out.
12. Having had a spiritual awakening as the result of these steps, we tried to carry this message to others in need, and to practice principles in all our affairs.

Map Marker #22

Only when you come to the end of yourself
does your life begin!

#2 REFRAME YOUR WEAKNESSES

To reframe your wickedness means to develop a sensitivity to that which keeps you from being and doing all that you were created to be and to do. This discipline or attitude builds right on top of the first—reaffirm your poverty. Once you have a right evaluation of your self, God, and others, you must be sensitive to anything that might pull you down or pull you away from being and doing what's right.

I see this as a mourning process. Learn to mourn over your weaknesses. I view weaknesses in two ways. First, your inner vulnerabilities that make you prone to fall apart or to do foolish things. Second, the trials you face when you suffer loss or when you are in the midst of your various problems.

You reframe your weaknesses by mourning—genuine mourning. By the way, when you mourn, you must feel the pain. Moan and groan over it! Feel it! Don't deny your feelings about it! The pain is for real, so really feel it! If you mourn properly, you'll discover something of a surprise on the other end. You will find a sense of comfort and inner joy.

Fortunately, or unfortunately, you don't need to look for problems and troubles—either generated by you or delivered to you. They have already been scheduled for your endurance! One of the primary growth factors in life is developing your muscle of endurance. When you reframe your weaknesses, you set yourself up for greater growth! So, don't waste your sorrows, reframe them!

#3 RENEW YOUR CONFIDENCE

To renew your confidence means is to develop a quiet, controlled strength. This discipline or attitude continues the progression. First, reaffirm your poverty (a right evaluation of your self, God, and others), then reframe your weaknesses (a sensitivity to that which keeps you from being and doing what you were created to be and to do), and now comes the renewing of your confidence—the renewal of your inner strength. In other words, once you see clearly who you really are, you are ready for growth. Then, if you are able to mourn over that which can keep you from growing, you actually graduate through the pile of problems. Now, you can't remain under the pile of mourning; you must gain inner strength as you emerge from the pile.

If you just learn how to mourn and remain there, you will be content to wallow in your weaknesses. Many people seem to enjoy suffering like this. They find a new friend in depression or loss or a sickness. They find that people seem to care more for them when

Map #5—Emotional RICHE$!   **167**

they're wallowing in a problem, so they take that problem on as their identity—sort of a badge of courage. Don't wallow in your sorrows! Mourn them! Recognize them! See them for what they are! And grow through it!

Another way to look at the progression is . . .

First, suffer the loss or problem with great sorrow!

Second, see the passing nature of the situation!

Third, stand on the promise of something better to come through it all!

To renew your confidence is to focus on the product of what you can learn in the midst of your struggles. It's developing a meekness—a quiet, controlled inner strength. It's learning to grow for it—no matter how rough or how tough life can be! Again, I say, it's not what happens to you, but how you handle what happens to you that matters most. Renew your confidence and live your life—inside out!

#4 REFOCUS YOUR HEART

To refocus your heart is to develop a passion for filling up the hole in your soul! Everybody is passionately seeking inner satisfaction. Note the progression of the first four attitudes. The first three speak primarily of that which is lacking within you and how you need to handle it. This fourth attitude or discipline is a kind of hungering and thirsting for what you want in your innermost being. This is that total satisfaction I was referencing earlier in this chapter.

I'll expand on it later, but here is an illustration of how your discontent works in your favor, if you allow it. The power of discontent provides the opportunity to refocus your heart! I see this power released as you take three positive steps:

First, *picture yourself as created by the Creator!* Although I've mentioned this earlier and probably will reference it again, you must not ignore this as one of the most powerful ingredients for your success. When you recognize your Creator, you avoid the temptation to play like you're God. This tends to keep you on track with who you really are and who you aren't. (This is the core of *reaffirm your poverty*.)

Second, *process the pain with the hope of something better to come!* The underlying attitude here is: All of the pain and disappointment will pass and are worth it, if I can get more inner satisfaction and growth for having experienced them. (This is the core of *reframe your weaknesses*.)

Third, *practice the presence of your Creator in your life!* This means to enjoy every day of your life from a different perspective—on a higher plane. It's living with your Creator as your partner in everything you do. There is a sense of accountability here that can't be achieved any other way. I have often taught with positive affirmation in the corporate marketplace that if you attempt to live your life without your Creator, you don't have prayer!

It's only when sensing your emptiness that you have access to spiritual fullness. These are the quiet cravings—the hungering and thirsting—for spiritual things, for the inner satisfaction of your soul! Refocus your heart!

INNER SELF	INNER SELF TOWARD OTHERS
Reaffirm Your Poverty	→ Reach Out With Compassion
Reframe Your Weaknesses	→ Relate as a Friend
Renew Your Confidence	→ Restore Peace
Refocus Your Heart	→ Rejoice In Persecution

Note that each of the attitudes or disciplines in the second column are dependent upon those in the first column. The first 4 speak of who you are on the inside and the second 4 have to do with how you relate to others—inside out.

*Map #5—Emotional **RICHE$!*** **169**

#5 REACH OUT WITH COMPASSION

To reach out with compassion is to treat everyone with grace and mercy! This means to identify with other's needs or plight in life in a compassionate way. Insert yourself into their shoes as best you can. Search for how you might best assist them. Initiate a positive effect toward the people in the world around you. Remember, whatever energy you give out, you receive it back at that very moment!

Reaching out with compassion is a source of healing for those you touch and for yourself, so that everyone gets better! Don't forget, this is not just an action toward another person; it's an attitude!

Reaffirm Your Poverty → REACH OUT WITH COMPASSION

For each of the attitudes or disciplines in the second list (INNER SELF TOWARD OTHERS) there is a corresponding attitude in the first list (INNER SELF). The INNER SELF attitudes are actually prerequisites for the INNER SELF TOWARD OTHERS attitudes.

Therefore, in order for you to be able to *reach out with compassion* you will do well to *reaffirm your poverty*. In other words, if you want to check out how you can reach out with compassion more effectively, start with reaffirming your poverty.

This makes so much sense when you think about it! It's very difficult to show compassion to another person, when you are filled with pride and haughtiness. On the other hand, when you are a person who has a right evaluation of your self, God and others, you are freed up to be able to show genuine compassion to others! When you have received grace from God, it's much easier to give out mercy!

#6 RELATE AS A FRIEND

To relate as a friend is to develop relationships where there is trust and love! Where there is trust and love, there is affirmation. Don't relate to others as friends for their approval. You don't want to give anyone that much power. You only seek approval from your Creator—your Higher Power. With friends, you must seek affirmation.

If you lead your life based on the good advice of others, who's life are you living? It's fine to look to others and listen to what they say, as long as you know deep in your gut that you are being true to who you are while you are seeking out their counsel and input. The question is do you trust your own counsel?

If you rise to your highest potential by learning to trust and love yourself, then what others think of you and your choices becomes less and less important.

Seeking the approval of others is a shallow pursuit, at best. There is little freedom and even less fulfillment. This is a path that can rob you of your joy and satisfaction. It kills little parts of you and is often the reason you are tempted to give away parts of yourself—the reason why you stop pursuing those things that reflect who you really are and what you really want!

Reframe Your Weaknesses → RELATE AS A FRIEND

The pre-requisite for *relate as a friend* is *reframe your weaknesses!* If you want to be more effective relating as a friend, you must check out how well you reframe your weaknesses. How is the mourning going? You can't be a good friend unless you have a lifestyle of being sensitive to your own weaknesses.

There are two critical cautions at this point: First, don't relate to another who is not into proper mourning! If you try to be a friend to a person who isn't sensitive to his weaknesses and therefore in denial, you may be in big trouble. Solomon warned that if you relate to a fool, you will end up living as a fool, too.

When a person hasn't reckoned with his/her weaknesses, he tends to want to point out yours in a condemnatory fashion.

Map #5—Emotional __RICHE$__!   171

Second, don't relate to another person without reframing your weaknesses! I have played the part of a fool on too many occasions. I have allowed people to use me to gain credibility that they lacked, allowed people to use me to pay for their own guilt by pointing out my failures, allowed wreckage to remain at the side of life's road, and allowed my naiveté to bring condemnation down upon me.

Without proper mourning you waste your sorrows and troubles, because without proper mourning there is no comfort and joy—satisfaction. And, without that satisfaction, you will find it very difficult to relate as a friend.

Everyone is in desperate need of the dynamic of friendship. Without a friendship you die. Life flows through it and death reigns without it!

#7 RESTORE PEACE

To restore peace is to develop peace within your sphere of influence wherever possible! Be a peacemaker—make peace where there is no peace. Search for trouble, distress, brokenness and those who are living in pieces. Listen to those around you. There is a great void out there—a great need to be understood.

In order to restore peace you must see the other person's strengths. This proves that you are listening and truly understand. Seek answers for what's best for this person. Do what you can do to promote peace-making—love, trust, and forgiveness. The world around you is in such desperate need of experiencing inner peace. When I even casually mention forgiveness in a seminar session, I notice the lightbulbs switching on throughout the audience. People are in great need for healing—for knowing inner peace!

The story is told in Spain of a father and his teenage son who had a relationship that had become strained. So the son ran away from home. His father, however, began a journey in search of his rebellious son. Finally, in Madrid, in a last ditch effort to find him, the father put an ad in the newspaper. The ad read: "Dear Paco, meet me in front of the newspaper office at noon. All is forgiven. I love you. Your father."

The next day at noon in front of the newspaper office over 800 "Pacos" showed up. They were all seeking forgiveness and love from their fathers. Believe me, there are massive amounts of Pacos out there looking for peace!

Renew Your Confidence → RESTORE PEACE

So, how can you best *restore peace* in the world around you? The pre-requisite is to *renew your confidence*—develop the attitude of meekness. Remember that meekness is a quiet, controlled inner strength. You don't have a chance to be a peacemaker without that quiet, controlled inner strength. You see, without that attitude of meekness you will have the tendency to be a reactor to people and things rather than be proactive, which is what restoring peace re-quires. Meekness is the inner strength that allows you to be a peace-maker! Restore peace and make people whole or remove yourself from this responsibility and leave the people around you in pieces. Choose to restore peace!

I like the simple prayer that says: "Dear Lord, as in the world I toil and through this world I flit. I pray make me a drop of oil and not a piece of grit!"

#8 REJOICE IN PERSECUTION

To rejoice in persecution is to develop the big picture on all troubles— especially the stresses that others bring upon you! Life is full of stress and distress. Many of life's stresses are circumstantial! I recently read: "You know it's a bad day when . . . the sun comes up in the West . . .

Map #5—Emotional RICHE$!   173

you jump out of bed and miss the floor . . . the bird singing outside your window is a buzzard . . . you put both contact lenses in the same eye . . . your pet rock snaps at you . . . the blind date turns out to be your ex-wife . . . your income tax refund check bounces . . . you put your bra on backwards and it fits better . . . Suicide Prevention puts you on hold."

Circumstantial stresses are terrible, but the most painful have to be the stresses that are caused by other people. The circumstantial are painful, but the people stresses are so miserably hurtful. It feels much like a betrayal!

Refocus Your Heart → REJOICE IN PERSECUTION

The pre-requisite that is necessary for you to *rejoice in persecution* is to *refocus your heart*! Your passion for filling up the hole in your soul—for genuine satisfaction and fulfillment—can set you up as a primary target for an onslaught of verbal persecution. When you begin to experience a sense of inner satisfaction and some level of fulfillment, you will find the jealousy and envy of others waiting to cut you down to their size—or lower!

Rejoice in persecution is the attitude that is necessary to stand up against this verbal barrage. The attitude is to take a bigger view of it all. Those who are verbally attacking you are hurting deeply within themselves. What is most encouraging is that they have noticed something about you. You are growing up! You are beginning to find a personal satisfaction that sets you apart! Your response must be to redouble your efforts to refocus your heart even more. You'll need it to truly rejoice in the midst of this kind of persecution! Keep hungering and thirsting for that inner, spiritual satisfaction for your soul! Then rejoice in persecution! This will drive your detractors nuts! Enjoy!

YOU ARE TO BE CONGRATULATED!

These 8 disciplines or attitudes are taken directly from the first seminar that Jesus gave on the hillside of the Sea of Galilee known as the Beatitudes. They all begin with "Blessed" which means to be congratulated or to be filled with happiness! Take on these attitudes and make them your primary disciplines of life! Meditate on them and discover the great depth within them! They offer you the ingredients that will produce the most valuable and powerful emotional riches you could ever experience!

"Blessed are the poor in spirit, for theirs is the kingdom of heaven.
Blessed are those who mourn, for they shall be comforted.
Blessed are the meek, for they shall inherit the earth.
Blessed are those who hunger and thirst for righteousness, for they shall be satisfied.
Blessed are the merciful, for they shall receive mercy.
Blessed are the pure in heart, for they shall see God.
Blessed are the peacemakers, for they shall be called sons of God.
Blessed are those who have been persecuted for the sake of righteousness, for theirs is the kingdom of heaven.
Blessed are you when {people} insult you and persecute you, and falsely say all kinds of evil against you because of Me.
Rejoice and be glad, for your reward in heaven is great; for in the same way they persecuted the prophets who were before you."

III. THE EMOTIONAL RICHES PICKUP . . .

THE TRUTH SHALL MAKE YOU FREE . . .

It's so easy to tell the truth about everyone else and so difficult to tell the truth about yourself. Yet trafficking in the truth about yourself may be at the heart of picking up your emotional riches!

Map #5—Emotional <u>RICHE$</u>!   175

Keith Miller, in his book, *The Secret Life of the Soul*, points out that when you are brutally honest about yourself to others three things happen . . .

First, you assist others in breaking through their denial! When another person shares a specific example of a character defect or self-centered behavior from his or her own life, that person becomes a mirror in which you may see yourself. You may actually see behind the wall of your denial. You may actually see things that you might never see by any other means—especially if you are preached to. Miller says, "I had been taught, like many religious people, that we, like the Pharisees, can't see the log in our own eye. But what they didn't teach me—even in seminary—was that preaching at people's denied sinful behaviors may only drive them further out of sight into denial. Instead of convincing the listeners to change, such preaching may only cause the listeners to recall other people's similar sins and prompt them to pray for those others to change." This is the favorite pastime of the church: confessing the sins of others.

Second, your inner voices of shame begin to shrink! When you begin to tell the truth about yourself, those gnawing voices that are filled with messages of 'shame on you' begin to weaken. You see, the only power they have on you is the threat that they might reveal who you really are—your failures, your character defects and your bad attitudes of your past. You really are as sick as your secrets! But when you voluntarily share these secrets in a safe setting, you loosen their strength and literally release their power over you! You weaken those voices to the point that they can do no damage to you any more.

Third, new inner voices of affirmation grow stronger! When you begin to open up the truth about yourself, revealing your secrets within a truth-telling group, you will begin to hear people say "Thanks so much for sharing today! It really meant a lot to me." "Thanks for being honest! We're so glad you are part of this community!" These words of affirmation are exactly what you need to make you stronger within yourself! As these voices of affirmation grow stronger, your shaming voices grow weaker. Think of it! These people who are now affirming you know the worst about you and yet still love you and are rewarding you for being so honest about your life. You are being affirmed for being yourself. You no longer have to put on an act!

Miller sums up truth-telling by saying, "To know that I could have voices inside arguing for me in the battles for self-esteem was wonderful news! I had seen early on as a child that I could never be perfect, but in truth-telling groups I saw that I can learn to become more honest. These loving, accepting voices were reparenting me, accepting me just as I am, by accepting my soul's halting attempts to be authentic. When those people, who had no manipulative stake in controlling me, really cared for me—imperfect as I admitted to being—I could begin to love myself! . . . when these new reparenting voices came inside my life, they began to change the balance of power in the inner warfare with the shaming voices that had tyrannized me as far back as I remember."

In order to pick up your emotional riches you must traffic in the truth about YOU! Then and only then will you be able to be truly free! I ran across this powerful piece about emotional happiness. The more I read it, the more I see about what it takes to be emotionally free . . .

Everybody Knows:
You can't be all things to all people.
You can't do all things at once.
You can't do all things equally well.
You can't do all things better than everyone else.
Your humanity is showing just like everyone else's.

Map #5—Emotional __RICHE$!__   **177**

So:

You have to find out who you are, and be that.

You have to decide what comes first, and do that.

You have to discover your strengths, and use them.

You have to learn not to compete with others,

Because no one else is in the contest of being you.

Then:

You will have learned to accept your own uniqueness.

You will have learned to set priorities and make decisions.

You will have learned to live with your limitations.

You will have learned to give yourself the respect that is due.

And you'll be a most vital mortal.

Dare To Believe:

That you are a wonderful, unique person.

That you are a once-in-all-history event.

That it's more than a right, it's your duty, to be who you are.

That life is not a problem to solve, but a gift to cherish.

And you'll be able to stay one up on what used to get you down.

Map Marker #68

Don't accept a counterfeit.
Be the best YOU that you can be!

Chapter 9

Map #6—Financial *RICHES!*

I. THE FINANCIAL RICHES PROBLEM . . .

At a hotel in downtown Chicago eight of the world's wealthiest men met. Together, these men controlled more money than the government of the United States at that time. Take a look at the list:

- The president of the largest independent steel company!
- The president of the largest gas company!
- The greatest wheat speculator!
- The president of the New York Stock Exchange!
- A member of the President's cabinet!
- One of the best on Wall Street!
- The head of the world's biggest monopolies!
- The president of the Bank of International Settlement!

These were, unquestionably, the most powerful, the most successful and wealthiest men ever gathered together! But when you examine what happened to these powerful men twenty-five years later, you get a clearer picture of what financial riches are all about.

Charles Schwab, the president of the largest independent steel company, lived on borrowed money for five years before he died in bankruptcy!

Howard Hopson, the president of the largest gas company, went insane!

Arthur Cutton, the greatest wheat speculator, died broke!

Richard Whitney, the president of the New York Stock Exchange, was sent to prison!

Albert Fall, a member of the President's cabinet, was pardoned from prison to die at home!

Jesse Livermore, one of Wall Street's best, committed suicide!

Ivar Krueger, the head of the greatest monopoly, committed suicide!

Leon Fraser, the president of the Bank of International Settlement, also committed suicide!

The world is filled with people who have been successful in accumulating money, but failed miserably in what I call the true financial riches that satisfy!

The financial riches problem is not how to accumulate riches—not how to make money. There are lots of resources on how to make more money. Some of the most popular would include Zig Ziglar, Tommy Hopkins, Anthony Robbins, Dennis Waitley et al. But note what their primary message is. All of these notables spend most of their time and material reminding you that you are the greatest source of riches. You are the most valuable asset you will ever have! Although, at any given time in your life, you may be in need of making more money, this is not your most critical problem with respect to finances.

Zig says it well: "If you strive for the quality of life first, standard of living invariably goes up; if you seek standard of living first, there is no guarantee that the quality of life will improve."

Map #6—Emotional <u>RICHE$</u>!   181

This same idea tracks with the map marker that speaks of how you can enrich your friends.

Map Marker #100

The greatest good we can do for others isn't
to share our riches with them, but to reveal theirs!

In other words, on your way to picking up your financial riches you must pick up all of the other riches or you won't be satisfied . . .

II. THE FINANCIAL RICHES PRINCIPLES . . .

The longer I live the more convinced I am that the essence of financial riches is not *the getting* of money and material things, but *the giving* of them away! I love this poem by Arthur William Beer:

> To get he had tried, yet his store was still meager.
> To a wise man he cried, in a voice keen and eager;
> "Pray tell me how I may successfully live?"
> And the wise man replied, "to get you must give."
>
> As to giving he said, "What have I to give?"
> I've scarce enough bread, and of course one must live;
> But I would partake of Life's bountiful store.
> Came the wise man's response; "Then you must give more."
>
> The lesson he learned; to get was forgotten,
> Toward mankind he turned with a love new begotten.
> As he gave of himself in useful living,
> Then joy crowned his days, for he grew rich in giving.

Map Marker #137

You make a living by what you get;
you make a life by what you give!

THE PRINCIPLE OF INSTANT RETURN

I have discovered a fascinating principle that may be the most dynamic and practical ever! Within the world of the intangible, there is an instant return on most every investment you make. When you show compassion to someone, you receive compassion right back. When you give love, you are loved. When you forgive, you enjoy a sense of forgiveness in your own soul. In the very act of giving something away, you immediately get it back.

So, it stands to reason that if you are lonely and feeling unloved, the power of solving that problem of loneliness is within you. You must show love to another in order to experience this wonder of love for yourself! If you are locked up in a pile of guilt in need of forgiveness, then you can begin the unlocking process by expressing genuine forgiveness to those in your world. You have the power to remain stuck in your loneliness or shake loose from it! You can remain in your pile of guilt or you can break free from it!

This same principle is active in the financial arena as well. If you are in need of more money, get into the practice of giving. Begin by looking around your house for what you might give away. Start with some of your junk that will prove to be real treasures for many people!

You'll be amazed at how good it feels to give things away! And, you will experience a new break-through, a shaking loose, a new freedom in your financial world!

Map #6—Emotional __RICHE$__!   183

A SPIRITUAL CONNECTION

Many quote the Bible by saying, "Money is the root of all evil!" However, this is a gross misquote. The verse actually says, "The love of money is the root of all evil!" The idea is that when you love money in such a way that you make it a god, you will serve it with all your might. And when you make your money your god, you make yourself vulnerable to every sort of evil! The most common evil tendency is to love money and use people.

The reverse is the spiritual connection: love people and use money! It's interesting to note that the most powerful principles that are quoted by the success 'experts' originate from the Bible. Now don't get this confused with the many religious-type, charlatans who misuse and misapply these principles for their own use and for the building of their own kingdoms. Don't judge the validity of the Biblical principles on finances by the spiritual weird-ones' use of them. That would be a little like judging Beethoven when listening to the Blanchester Junior High Band!

The Bible is full of life-changing principles regarding your financial riches. Over 2000 verses teach what to do with your riches—how to accumulate, give, save and invest! Two out of three parables taught by Jesus have to do with how to handle your financial riches so that you can be truly rich! Even as you read the thousands of biographies and stories, you can readily see that many of the Biblical characters are people who have accumulated significant financial riches.

THE GOD TEST!

One of the most incredible teachings from the Bible has to do with putting the God of gods to the test! Throughout the Bible it's clear that no one is ever to test God. How can the creature put the Creator to the test in any area? It's unthinkable!

However, within the writings of the Jewish prophet, Malachi, God, the Creator, invites you to put Him to a test. This test is in regard to your money. It says, " . . . test Me now in this," says the LORD of hosts, "if I will not open for you the windows of heaven and pour out for you a blessing until it overflows." In brief, this test consists of your giving a percentage (a tithe) of what you earn to God. Note that I didn't say to give it to me or to your church or to you synagogue or to your favorite religious ministry. The principle is to give some percentage of your income to God. Giving to God is giving a percentage of your income to your Higher Power and His higher causes—whatever you consider them to be! Given this definition, then, you may choose to give your money through some organization—church, synagogue, etc.

There are two promises that go along with this unusual test. First, *overflowing blessing to you*! This goes right back to the principle of instant return. Second, *protection from those things that devour your finances*—"Then I will rebuke the devourer for you . . . " Check out the destroyers of your finances. When you are into the principle of giving, you will not only experience great blessing but also you'll be given a certain protection against your money devourers! Try it out! Test God out! It's been my personal experience that most dramatic results occur, when a person dares to be a giver!

There are four principles to guide your thinking about your financial riches:

First, you are a steward of your financial riches! You came into this world with nothing—absolutely naked—and you will go out in the same mode! What you now have or what you may soon accumulate are only yours for a short period of time.

My personal approach is to view everything as belonging to God and nothing belonging to me. This puts my riches in a wonderful, yet dynamic, perspective. I am the manager of the riches that I now

Map #6—Emotional <u>RICHE$</u>!   **185**

have and what I will have in the future. This is a stewardship responsibility that I am given while on planet earth. I believe that I am held accountable in some way for how I manage what I've been given. This not only applies to financial riches, but to all of the other riches as well. For instance, I have been given the precious treasures of my wife, my five children, my sons and daughters in law, my two grand-children, my friends and other extended family members. I have been given the responsibility of managing these relationships well. I don't own them, but they are in the realm of my personal stewardship!

This sums it up:

> You are not the Creator, but the creature!
> You are not the Designer, but the distributor!
> You are not the Master, but the manager!

Second, enjoy the blessings that come your way! Don't spend time bemoaning what you don't have. Spend your time enjoying what you do have. There is no greater attitude than that of gratitude! Grateful people live their lives more fully. Grateful people live their lives more wisely. Grateful people live their lives more successfully. Grateful people really know how to live!

Third, evaluate all you have accumulated! Take an inventory of all of your riches. Don't miss anything! Then evaluate how you are either using or enjoying them. You see, riches are meant to be in circulation as much as possible. Riches are meant to be used and enjoyed. Those who bury them lose them all! Those who use them will enjoy even greater riches in the process!

Fourth, prepare to give them away! Keep your riches flowing! Oh, I know what you may be thinking; that your cashflow seems to be flowing, but mostly out and not in! What I'm suggesting to you is that you throw yourself into this powerful principle of giving more and more.

Get into giving! I'm convinced that you are the one who benefits the most from your giving!

Give to people's needs around you! Look for those needs and do what you can do to meet them.

Give no matter your circumstances! You can only give some portion of what you have in your possession. Set a percentage and go for it!

Give quietly without making a show about it! If you give in order to be seen as a giver, then you lose the dynamic of the principle of instant return on your investment. Give quietly and enjoy it immensely!

Look for the needs!

There is no lack of need in the world for your giving pleasure. Needs are everywhere! In fact, it has been proven over and over that charitable giving from the private sector can be enormously effective in meeting community and world-wide needs. In fact, charitable giving through the private sector outshines the billions of dollars given through the many, wasteful, administratively-burdened, government programs. And, charitable giving through the private sector tends to have a little higher touch to it. Therefore, the whole encounter is more powerful for everyone involved—for the giver and for the givee!

Look into how much of your gift goes to the need!

Always inquire what the administrative costs are within the organization through which you are giving your money or gifts. In too many organizations there is a higher percentage of your gift going to pay administrative costs than there is going to the stated need. If you want to pay people to run charitable organizations and you don't care

Map #6—Emotional __RICHE$__! 187

how effective the organization is, it's easy to do. But, remember, you are a steward, so seek to be as effective as possible in your giving!

I have recently become aware of a wonderful charity that is doing a miraculous work for the destitute poor. **FOOD FOR THE POOR** was created in 1982 by Ferdinand Mahfood, a gifted businessman with a big heart for those in need and specific skills in the import/export business. His mission is to help the poorest of the poor—the destitute—through an existing (and ever-growing) network of clergy and spiritual-based social ministries. **FOOD FOR THE POOR** provides whatever this network requests to properly feed, educate, house and minister to the poor. By buying goods in bulk, accepting quality gifts-in-kind, and thoroughly understanding the import/export business, **FOOD FOR THE POOR** meets these needs at the lowest possible cost. To date FFP has shipped more than $400 million worth of food, clothing, medical and educational supplies, building materials and self-help tools to those in greatest need, while maintaining a low 9.2% rate for all administrative and fund-raising costs! FFP has been ranked as one of the top most-efficient charities in America! (Check out my website for additional information: http://www.timtimmons.com.)

Look into the strategic nature of the charity's mission!

There are many fine charitable organizations and they are just that—fine charitable organizations who are effective at raising funds. But what are they doing? A guideline that is most attractive to me is: *Give a man a fish and he'll eat for a day; teach him how to fish and he'll eat for a lifetime*! Look to give your riches to charities that are using their resources as a 'seeding' for the multiplication of the gift. For instance, you can hand out food or you can grow food. You can give out tanks of water or you can dig wells. You can give furniture or you can build furniture manufacturing plants. You can give clothes or you can teach them how to make clothes for themselves. Usually the wisest approach is to give them water and to help them dig the well to perpetuate your gift! Look for organizations that are thinking in this way as much as possible! Are they being strategic and effective?

Look to be creative in your giving!

There's a new and wonderful concept that has created a whole new way to give to your favorite charity! You can use your normal purchases of various goods and services and give to your favorite charity or cause at the same time—at no extra cost! **The Institute for Charitable Giving** (referenced at my website) has devised a program by which you can purchase quality products such as internet service providers, telephone service, restaurants and dining, full-service travel, self-help books and tapes, accounting services, apartment rentals, architecture and interior design, legal services, cars, trucks, vans, mini-vans and utility sports vehicles (purchase or lease), dry-cleaners, employment career placement, seminars, energy savings, environmental product, home repair and remodeling, telecommunications (residential and business), magazine subscription and renewals, mortgage loans and refinancing, printing, real estate brokers, retirement development, electricity and energy, and almost any consumer benefit you can imagine! When you purchase these goods and services, a portion of what you pay is directed into the charity of your choice! This is more of a passive way to get into giving, but your favorite charity doesn't mind. The worthy cause that they are championing is enhanced by every dollar that flows into their organization. Check it out! It's a wonderful way to get into a lifestyle of giving more effectively!

III. THE FINANCIAL RICHES PICKUP . . .

On your way to financial riches you must pick up all of your riches or you will not enjoy what you are able to accumulate. Pick-

Map #6—Emotional RICHE$! 189

ing up your financial riches may be the most simple of all of the riches. It all boils down to three basics:

GET ALL YOU CAN GET . . .

GIVE ALL YOU CAN GIVE . . .

BE GRATEFUL FOR ALL YOU HAVE . . .

Chapter 10

Map #7—Spiritual *RICHES!*

When I speak of spiritual riches, I am not talking about religion. Religion destroys people with its grip. In fact, in the name of religious causes masses of people are literally being murdered daily throughout the world! No, I'm not talking about religion. Even Jesus told the religious of his day that they were "snakes" and "painted tombstones." He was down on religion and so am I.

Years ago, when I wanted to obtain my "ticket" to get into heaven, religion told me that there were, at least, 15 things that I couldn't do. As I looked over the list, immediate depression set in. Many of these were my goals in life! Not only did it all seem depressing to me, it was also boring!

Then I ran into a religious group that said that all I had to do to get my ticket was to let them dunk me in their tank. (This sacrament comes in a variety of methods—immersion, sprinkling, pouring, squirting, or hosing them down.) The only thing I gained from that experience was a wet body.

Religion blindly accepts a certain system of do's and don'ts and ignores more basic issues. Therefore, religion can make your life quite miserable. It's comparable to a sedative given to a dying person. It may make him feel better, but he's still dying!

In my own spiritual search to know God, I finally came to understand that there is a supernatural factor in our world that I was forced to examine. As I worked through the evidence for this supernatural factor, I discovered that God is knowable and you don't have to shelve your brain in the process of searching.

The supernatural factor isn't a blind or mystical leap in the dark, hoping to find meaning to life. It's based upon evidence, logic and good common sense. Check out my website for more information about THE SUPERNATURAL FACTOR, and consider it for yourself!

I. THE SPIRITUAL RICHES PROBLEM . . .

Have you noticed that the most frequent entrance that God makes on the scene in the affairs of mankind is in the midst of man's troubles? On the one hand, God is accused of being the cause of all disasters. And, on the other hand, God is the source of most everyone's desperate appeal through prayer when facing disease or distress. In other words, most people's tendency is to look to God when in a crisis, then to leave Him out in the continual.

Map Marker #37

Sign in Nebraska high school building:
"In the event of an earthquake or tornado,
the Supreme Court ruling against prayer
in school will be temporarily suspended."

Map #7—Spiritual RICHE$! 193

In the continual, day to day routine of life there is a natural tendency to trivialize God. I have observed, at least, three ways that we all tend to trivialize. **First, we tend to make God one of the many!** Whatever you make your highest priority and focus, you tend to make your idol or your god. Therefore, we tend to worship several gods in our lives—money, cars, house, loved ones, job, power, position, sex, or whatever your drug of choice may be! If you keep the God of gods your primary focus, then all other priorities are held in a balanced perspective.

The first of the Ten Commandments speaks to this— "You shall have no other gods before Me!" There are three possible meanings to "before"—no other gods *in front of* (ahead of) Me, no other gods *instead of* Me, and no other gods *in the face of* Me.

Second, we tend to make God more accessible! We attempt to make God more localized, down-sizing Him so that we can touch Him, see Him, bargain with Him, bow down to Him and control Him in any way for our purposes and desires. We tend to think that we can package God into a symbol, an altar, a building, a picture, a statue, or a piece of jewelry. This is what is meant by the second Commandment—"You shall not make for yourself an idol, or any likeness of what is in heaven . . . you shall not worship them or serve them." Any kind of idol (graven image) tends to trivialize the God of gods down to just another god!

Map Marker #203

God is not a cosmic bellboy for whom we can press a button whenever we need something!

Third, we tend to make God in our image! In the early chapters of the Scriptures, jointly accepted by the Jewish, Moslem and Christian traditions, it is said that we are created "in the image of God." We tend to twist this around and make God in "our image"—making God think, feel and do the ways we think, feel and do! Dan McCollough, in his fine book, **The Trivialization of God**, suggests that we tend to embrace four popular deities: the God-of-my-cause, the God-of-my-understanding, the God-of-my-experience, and the God-of-my-cure. Instead of serving God by working for a just cause, we want to serve a just cause by using God. We begin with a cause, then re-conceive God around that cause—and the same with our understanding, our experiences and our cures. We tend to fit God into our denominational flavor or our doctrinal persuasion. I am convinced that the awesome God of gods has no interest in being a bapterian, an episcolic, or a presbytist! He doesn't want to join! You see, He's God!

Map Marker #108

If God is small enough for us to understand,
He isn't big enough for us to worship!

This is exactly what gets in the way of picking up your spiritual riches. The pre-requisite for becoming spiritually wealthy is to join and contribute to one of a variety of religious organizations, all claiming to be the legitimate, possibly the only, genuine franchise that God has set up on planet earth!

Map #7—Spiritual RICHE$! 195

Map Marker #54

Some people are willing to serve God, but only
in an advisory capacity!

In order to pick up your spiritual riches you are going to want to get the big picture!

II. THE SPIRITUAL RICHES PRINCIPLES . . .

Your spiritual riches directly affect all of the other six riches! This is why it is symbolized as the bottomline in the way I spell riches . . .

R-I-C-H-E-$

Spiritual riches provide
- . . . meaning for your relational riches
- . . . wisdom for your intellectual riches
- . . . direction for your career riches
- . . . energy for your health riches
- . . . inspiration for your emotional riches
- . . . balance for your financial riches

Map Marker #41

Practicing psychiatry without faith in God is like
meeting a hungry man and giving him a toothpick!

IS YOUR GOD TOO SMALL?

When you look up into the sky at night, you can get a bigger picture on what the God of gods is all about. There are 100 billion stars in our galaxy and our galaxy is located in a universe of 100 billion other galaxies! The scientific community of astral physicists are producing more and more literature noting the incredible design of the universe which begs for an intelligent designer. Take your choice: blind chance that requires multitudes of universes or design that requires only one. Many scientists, when they admit their views, are arguing on the side of a Designer. One scientist in the field of mathematical physics said that he has to go to the philosophy department in order to find a good atheist for a debate, because the physics department isn't much use anymore!

The universe of stars demonstrates a magnitude charted out by the Designer. On the other hand, the brain contains 75-100 billion nerve cells. Each of these nerve cells can have up to 10,000 connections. Go figure. Is this a result of pure chance or does it speak of some sort of purposeful detail of a Designer?

Just how big is your God? How high is your Higher Power?

Is your God too small or is He AWESOME? To know the awesome God, you must acknowledge what you don't know. To see the light of God, you must pass through the dark night of your soul. To gain faith, you must begin with doubt. To hear a Word from God, you must wait through the silences of God. To experience the comfort of God, you must experience the misery of life!

BABY STEPS OF FAITH

Whatever your spiritual bent, I want to encourage you to search it out for yourself. And in your search to make sense out of the spiritual riches of life, be sure to focus your search on the truth about the

Map #7—Spiritual <u>RICHE$</u>!   **197**

God of gods. The God of gods is the only possible way to put your life in a perspective that is true to life as it is and people as they are!

Map Marker #20

No man can truly stand erect until he has first bent his knee to the God of gods!

I want to recommend a book for your consideration to assist you in your search for the God of gods. I have found it to be a most important tool for those who are honestly searching to sort out what life is all about! Get it! Read it! Underline it! Do your best to understand its implications for your life right now! The book is **The Universe Next Door** by James W. Sire. (http://www.timtimmons.com)

By the way, if there is a God of gods out there, then you ought to be able to go direct. It's been my experience that anyone who goes direct finds what they're looking for. It works like this. One of my best friends is an intellectual sort. He requires proof, no matter what the issue! He decided to put the God of gods to the test. He began to read the bible. He started reading Proverbs, the Psalms, and then added Matthew, Mark, Luke and John. Everyday he read a little. But he didn't just read. He prayed a simple prayer. "Dear God. If you're for real, I want to know you. I want to plug into you. I want to learn how to be and do all that you created me to be and do!"

Within the first month of this experiment he learned some things, but it was only an intellectual exercise. By the end of the second month he found that he felt good about this new discipline. Within the third month he had a simple wake-up call. In the midst of a painful relational loss he found himself naturally turning his life over to the God of gods. And in this turning over he found a new faith and a new peace that everything was going to be all right. This was more than 30 years ago and he has built his life around this God of gods ever since. You would never think of this man as a religious man, but he is deeply spiritual and enjoys his riches more enthusiastically than most anyone I have ever known! He has the true riches and he knows the source of the greatest riches of all!

III. THE SPIRITUAL RICHES PICKUP . . .

Faith is the key to picking up your spiritual riches. "Now faith is the assurance of things hoped for; the conviction of things not seen." Through the power of believing many miraculous things are achieved. Through faith you pick up your customized spiritual riches.

Possibly the greatest benefit that comes from picking up your spiritual riches is hope! Hope is another form of faith! Hope is ever-present when you plug yourself into your Higher Power. A few years ago I discovered three revolutionary promises of hope that have become life-changing in thousands of people's lives! I have never experienced anything more powerful than these! Faith is a verb—a verb that is filled with hope!

PROMISE 1—The Promise of Good Endings!

This first promise goes like this: "God causes all things to work together for good to those who love God, to those who are called according to His purpose." The promise here is that no matter what happens, all things, through your Higher Power, are worked *together* with something else for your good. If you are plugged into the God of gods, you can count on the fact that He will work all of the bad things that come into your life together with other things, so that good will result for you!

Map #7—Spiritual __RICHE$!__   **199**

A death within your sphere of family and friends . . . that very sad and damaging divorce . . . the financial crisis . . . the automobile accident . . . the loss of your job . . . the betrayal of a friend . . . the ravages of cancer . . . heart disease . . . *all of these things will be worked together with something else for your good!* What an incredible promise!

PROMISE 2—The Promise of Great Escapes!

The second promise is articulated in the following way: "No temptation has overtaken you but such as is common to man; and God is faithful, who will not allow you to be tempted beyond what you are able, but with the temptation will provide the way of escape also, so that you will be able to endure it." There are three observations that are most important in making this promise yours.

First, *you are not the only person who has gone through your troubles*— "but such as is common to man." One of the great comforts of life is knowing that others are going through the same thing as you are. When you think you are the only one who has ever experienced these particular problems or as bad as they seem to be, you can be overwhelmed by your circumstances.

Second, *no matter how bad your troubles are, God will provide a way of escape!* The image here is a person who is hemmed in by mountains of problems all around him and sees no way out. He feels overwhelmed and trapped! However, in this desperate situation God will provide a mountain pass to get through it! You can count on it! There will always be a way out!

Third, *your way out of your overwhelming problems—your way of escape—does not bail you out of your problem-situation, but leads you directly through it!* Most everyone would choose the bail-out option for getting them out of their problems. However, this promise has nothing to do with bailing you out, but everything to do with getting you through. You see, the best way out of your problems is to go through them! When faced in an impossible situation, the God of gods will give you the strength and wisdom to get through it! *The best way out is through*!

PROMISE 3—The Promise of Great Expectations!

The third powerful promise is: "I am confident of this, the good work that your Creator set in motion within you, He will not leave undone, but complete it." Whatever mission you were created to do will be alive in you until you die! You can be confident that your Creator is still very proactive in your life! You can count on it!

I live by these three promises every day of my life and they work! When I live my life with these promises in mind, I am better able to keep it in mind that there is a God of gods out there and I am not Him!

Map Marker #35

People always get into trouble when they think they can handle their lives without God!

WHAT IF GOD

What if God couldn't take the time to bless us today because we couldn't take the time to thank Him yesterday?

What if God decided to stop leading us tomorrow because we did not follow Him today?

What if we never saw another flower bloom because we grumbled when God sent the rain?

What if God didn't walk with us today because

Map #7—Spiritual <u>*RICHE$!*</u>   201

we failed to recognize it as His day?

What if God took away the Bible tomorrow because
we would not read it today?

**What if God took away His message because
we failed to listen to His messenger?**

What if the door of the church was closed because
we did not open the door of our heart?

**What if God stopped loving and caring for us because
we failed to love and care for others?**

What if God would not hear us today because
we would not listen to Him yesterday?

**What if God answered our prayers the way
we answer His call for service?**

What if God met our needs the way
we give Him our lives???

Map Marker #81

Those who go against the grain of God's law
shouldn't complain when they get splinters!

Recently, I discovered 6 steps that are the most effective action-steps I have ever encountered! Try these out as you pick up your spiritual riches . . .

Step #1—OBSERVE *God's creation—everyday!* Too much time is spent in the concrete jungle without noticing and appreciating the creation—trees, flowers, oceans, lakes, mountains, stars, moon, sunrises and sunsets. Get into the wonders of God's creation!

Step #2—OPEN *yourself up to God's work within you—everyday!* God wants to partner with you throughout your life. Practice His presence with you wherever you are. When you get up in the morning instead of saying, "Good God, it's morning!", say "Good morning, God!" Listen to the promptings of your Creator in your gut. And as long as it is not illegal, immoral or fattening, go for it!

Step #3—OFFER *your body to God—everyday!* After you say "Good morning, God!", then ask, "What do you have for me to do today?" This is an act of making yourself available, which gets you outside of yourself and away from wallowing in your own problems!

Step #4—OVERHAUL *your mind—everyday!* Don't be fit into the mold of going along with the herd. Be transformed—changed inside out—by the renewing of your mind!

Step #5—OBTAIN *a servant's heart—everyday!* Don't think more highly of yourself than you ought to think. Show a genuine interest in others' needs and do what you can to contribute toward meeting those needs! And, as you reach out to others in this way, you will receive it back to you directly! Such a deal!

Step #6—OPERATE *with a supportive group—everyday!* Don't attempt to live your life alone. Remember the geese that fly in a V formation. And, remember the banana: once he left the bunch he was skinned!

These daily steps are dynamic and life-changing, if you allow them to be! If you are a believer in the God of gods, you will get to know Him better. If you aren't sure of this God of gods, these steps may lead you to Him! Either way, you can't lose! Do the steps!

The Book of Ecclesiastes in the Bible is a most fascinating treatise on life. Solomon's thesis is simple. All is empty—like a vapor! No matter what it is, you'll find that most everything in life cannot bring you happiness and joy. Solomon does, however, point out that there are two primary things you can do that will produce some sense

Map #7—Spiritual RICHE$! 203

of inner joy and peace. First, *fear God and keep His commandments*! This is simply a constant acknowledgment on your part that you believe and revere the God of gods as your Higher Power. Second, *enjoy His blessings every day*! Remember, your past is a canceled check and your future is a promissory note. All you have is your present—today! Be grateful and enjoy the many blessings you are given each and every day! **These two acts alone may bring about a spiritual change in your life and make you a very wealthy person**!

Pick up your spiritual riches—everyday!

I love the prayer of the little girl. She sincerely asked for many things and expressed several concerns. Then, she finished with "And, by the way, God, please take care of yourself, cause if you get sick, we're all sunk!

Chapter 11

The Power of Deciding

If there are 5 birds sitting on a log and 3 of them decide to fly away, how many birds are left on the log? There are still 5. Just because you decide to fly away doesn't mean that you will! Decisions don't insure action, but there will be no action without a decision. And, there will be no wise actions without wise decisions!

Turn Your Wants Into Goals!

Your wants reflect your life purpose or vision for your life! Your purpose statement becomes more and more critical. Have you written it down yet? You may have revised it several times and probably will some more as you grow. However, the most important thing is to get it down. This is your life statement!

Once you have settled upon your life statement as best you can, you are ready to write your mission statement. This is turning your wants (life statement) into goals (mission statement). Your life statement is your overall purpose or calling in life; your mission statement is what you are going to do to fulfill your purpose or calling in life.

Now take your wants that you listed under each of the seven riches and turn them into goals—short mission statements. To begin, focus on just one of the riches. Finish the process on one and then move to another.

Goals are discovered by answering three questions:

#1- What are the steps necessary to fulfill this want? What is it going to take to get what I want? Be brutally honest with as much detail as possible. No want is going to appear just by the wanting. Don't worry about how many or how few steps you have listed. Don't be afraid to change them as you go. You are a work in progress!

#2- What do I need to have or to do to reach each step? There is a Murphy's Law that reminds me often of a grim, but important, reality:

Map Marker #66

Whenever you start out to do
something, you discover
that three other things must be done first!

No matter how you try to avoid this reality, you can't. You may need to obtain a certain amount of money . . . to acquire some education . . . time . . . read . . . some sort of certification or licensing . . . skills . . . mentors or key contacts. Whatever it is that you need, you must write it down. Otherwise, you don't know or tend to forget what you're looking for.

#3- When do I want to accomplish each step and each want? Now you get to the crucial area of timing. This is the most fluid and dynamic of all so far. Since there are so many moving parts to your

wants and needs, you may find it difficult to nail down the dates as firmly as you might like. It's easy to be discouraged, when a date or deadline is missed. Don't crater over having to move your dates around. You are normally not in total control of your circumstances or they wouldn't be called circumstances. And, you are not normally in control of other people that you need to accomplish what you want.

This brings me to a very important subject. Do everything you can NOT to become too dependent upon others to accomplish your wants! It's too easy to depend upon others to fulfill your calling and then, it's too easy to blame them for not 'coming through', instead of facing the reality that you didn't come through. Set up your life so that you are in as much control of your destiny as possible. Then, you only have you to count on, to blame and to reward!

The answers to these three questions have now become decisions that are ready for action! Don't be timid about aiming too high. Higher goals tend to stretch you toward doing greater and better things. When you are inspired by a great purpose, all your thoughts break their shackles. Your mind leaps beyond your limitations, your consciousness expands in every way and you find yourself in a great and wonderful world. Dormant faculties and talents become alive and you discover yourself to be a greater person by far than you ever dreamed to be.

Map Marker #55

Failure does not come because
you aimed too high and missed it,
but that you aimed too low and hit it!

FOUR DECISIONS TO KEEP YOU GOING

At this point you probably have good intentions to follow-through on picking up and possessing all of your riches for your personal enjoyment. Good intentions will not get you what you want! I want to share with you four decisions that will boost you along your way toward all of the riches you want.

Map Marker #17

Even if you're on the right road,
you can still be run over, if you stop!

#1-A Mission Decision: Pursue Your <u>RICHE$</u>!

This is the most obvious, but must be stated. This is your personal roadmap to riches. It's like taking a bath. You must do it yourself!

There are three depressing facts that, if understood, can move you toward taking personal responsibility in pursuing your riches. First, *no one is as excited about what you're doing as you are!* Don't wait for others to be as excited as you are. This is your deal—your pursuit! Remember, as an adult, you don't need anyone's approval. It would be very nice to get affirmation from others, but not their approval. You set yourself up for major pain and disappointment, if you think you need someone's approval.

Second, *there is no meeting going on right now in which a group of people is discussing how to make your life more successful!* Now, they may be meeting and they may be talking about you, but I can assure you that this was not the subject. You must face up to the fact that no one lives and breathes just to make your life work better. This brings us to the third, and for some, the most depressing of all!

Third, *if anything good is going to happen to you, you must make it happen!* Make sure you own this fact—YOU MUST DO IT YOUR-SELF!

This doesn't negate the good that others may do on your behalf nor does it negate the daily blessings you experience from your God!

A long time ago I was told a story about a farmer who turned a desolate piece of land right behind his house into a beautiful garden. When the vegetation grew into a gorgeous green, he invited his priest out to see this wonderfully lush garden.

When the priest walked into the garden, he was overwhelmed. He said, "Look at the corn! It's beautiful! God sure does make good corn!" He continued on, "Wow, look what God grew here . . . look at those beans and tomatoes! Isn't God something!" The farmer had about all he could take. The priest had totally ignored the hard work the farmer had put into this garden to make it what it had become. The farmer could take no more and said, "Father, I wish you could have seen this garden when God was working it by Himself!" You do your part based upon God doing His part. You do the possible by faith that God will do the impossible!

#2-A Maturity Decision: Persevere!

Maturity occurs when you break through the walls of frustration. The best way out is through! I love Charlie Brown's response as he was stressing out one night: "Sometimes I lie awake at night and I ask, 'Where have I gone wrong?' Then a voice says to me, 'This is going to take more than one night.'" No matter how tough the situation is that you face, there is growth on the other side of this wall of frustration and pain. Failure has been identified as the path of least persistence!

Don't try to avoid the obstacles that present themselves to you. If you avoid them now, you must face them later. If you face them now, you can enjoy growth and maturity later! ***The best way out is through!***

#3-A Mastermind Decision: Participate In A Group!

I said it earlier in a different way, but it's impossible to overemphasize it. You must participate in a group! Operating as the Lone Ranger will not produce the riches that are yours! I have found great strength, wisdom and balance within a group for the last 27 years.

I presently meet with a group of four other men on a weekly basis. We call it an ACTION GROUP. Each week we meet for coffee or for lunch for one hour. There are two primary purposes for our little group. First, *it is a mainstay of support!* We can lean on one another. Everyone gets a turn at trials and troubles. Most must suffer through them alone, surviving the best they can—under the circumstances! Through a group like this, you experience these same trials and troubles with the support that each person brings. Most of the time, one of the members of the group has gone through something similar. The wisdom of personal experience and survival is invaluable! This kind of support can empower you to not remain under the circumstances, but on top of them! Second, *it is a motivation toward success!* Our goal is not just to survive, but to thrive! It's been within the dynamics of groups such as this that I have been moved to a higher level of success—whether it be personal, relational, professional, or just working my way over another of life's hurdles!

#4-A Mentoring Decision: Pass It On!

Nothing teaches you better than when you are responsible to teach someone else! When you share your experience with another person, it makes an indelible mark on your psyche. There is something about the sharing process that enables you to better articulate what you think, what you feel and what you intend to do.

Over the years I have had the privilege of being mentored and mentoring others. When I first understood its total value, I was humbled by the process! In the late 1970's I was approached by a very talented young man who wanted me to teach him how to speak more effectively. I took on the project, feeling confident and adequate for the task. I knew I had something to give him that was very valuable and would make a significant mark on his life and livelihood. I was ready to play the role of helping this young man to better his skills and his trade. I was kind of proud of the fact that he had sought me out. I figured that he definitely made a wise choice in choosing me as his mentor in this area!

But I came to realize that I was woefully missing the point of this mentoring dynamic. I was not prepared for what I was about to experience through the many hours of intense interaction with my mentoree. Oh, I taught him, alright, and I know he appreciated what I was able to give him. The surprise was what happened to me!

I found that through the mentoring process I, the mentor, was learning so much more about me and my expertise. Through mentoring I was mastering the material that I already knew! Now through this process, what I *knew* was quickly becoming what I *own*. Through this mentoring process I now possessed what I used to just profess to know.

What an thrilling process! Now I look for people to mentor, knowing that no matter what they might gain from the process, I will become truly wealthy through the experience!

PASS IT ON so that you might possess it for yourself!

Chapter 12

The Power of Doing

After all is said and done, there is more said than done! Once you have entered into the power of decision-making, you are faced with the reality that remains—the doing! I want to assist you in going from the deciding to doing to done! Make sure to use the tapes as a constant reminder of what you are doing and make use of your workbook. The workbook is designed to help you create a personal business plan—*a plan that you can adopt for the rest of your life!*

I want to give you three more sticks of dynamite that contain the power to move from decision to done. Check them out and work them out by the use of your workbook.

The Power of Dreaming . . .

We have known for years that the power of a thought, an idea or a dream is unstoppable! There is no doubt that "What you can conceive and believe you can achieve!" The power of an idea brought down the Berlin Wall, which surprised the world with its speed, once the timing was right. The dream of running a sub-four minute mile, the dream of launching into space, and the dream that overcomes a disability are only isolated incidents whereby a dream became more powerful than the greatest obstacles! Don't be afraid to dream!

WHAT ARE YOUR DREAMS?

The Power of Discontent . . .

Life is filled with disappointment, discouragement, disaster, disease and unimaginable, painful difficulties. You have a choice. *You can choose to be overwhelmed by them or you can choose to overcome them!* Being overwhelmed may not even qualify as a choice, since these things are naturally overwhelming to most any human. Maybe the choice is between staying overwhelmed or choosing to overcome them.

If you want to overcome them, you have a terrific motivating factor built-in to these negative, deadly influences and events. It's the power of discontent! When you come to the point of not wanting to wallow in the pain any longer, you arrive at a strategic destination—*enough is enough!* You can be motivated and launched into the next step through your discontent! Use it to your advantage! Otherwise, this same discontent will slowly destroy you.

BUILD ON YOUR DISCONTENT!

The Power of Dying to a Dream . . .

There is one more reality that I want to leave with you. Most dreams don't work out as originally planned! Dreams get shattered by the circumstances of life! Dreams get shot down by others— friends and enemies! Dreams get shelved by being crowded out by other more 'urgent' matters! Dreams get short-circuited by the unforeseen!

I have come to the conclusion that all dreams will experience a death of some sort. The important thing is to be in control of this death experience. When a dream dies, many good things happen in this painful process!

- Your perspective can be reframed!
- Your personness can be refined!
- Your purpose can be refocused!
- Your passion can be rekindled!
- Your personal power can be recharged!

In other words, through the dying process, your dream can become re-designed and redeveloped into a greater dream—more realistic, more relational, and more responsible! This has been my experience in the counseling room as well as in my own life! You have to die to your dream in order to have it resurrected back to life—this time, it's better!

How many times have you known a single lady who has finally given up on ever being married. Once she announces that she has died to her dream living with her prince in a cute, little house with a white picket fence, the man of her dreams walks into her life! But he is so much better than she had ever dreamed!

Or how about the lady who has dreamed of having her own children, but never able to do so. After going through the medical gymnastics to overcome this problem of infertility, she comes to the end of her rope. After dying to the thought of ever having her own children, she relents to the idea of adopting a child instead. She died to her lifelong dream! Then, a few months after receiving her new adopted baby, she mysteriously and miraculously becomes pregnant! Now, in just a few months, she will have a house full of kids! Don't be discouraged with the death of your dream. Go ahead and die to it yourself! Your dream must die in order to be ready for the resurrection!

ALLOW YOUR DREAMS TO DIE!

**Your Roadmap to RICHE$ is a game plan for making
the REST of your life the BEST of your life!
YOU CHOOSE!**

A little bird was flying south for the winter. It was so cold it froze up and fell to the ground in a barnyard. While it was lying there, a cow came by and dropped some manure on it. As it lay there in the pile of manure, it began to realize how warm it was. The manure was actually thawing him out! He lay there all warm and happy, and soon began to sing for joy. The farmer, walking by, heard the bird chirping and saw that it was stuck and couldn't get out of the dried manure. So, he set out to free the bird. The bird jumped out and an hour later this little bird froze to death!

There are three morals to the story:

1. Not everyone who gets you into a mess is your enemy.
2. Not everyone who gets you out of a mess is your friend.
3. For goodness sake, when you're in a mess up to your neck, don't sing about it!

MORE PRODUCTS BY TIM TIMMONS

- ❑ **Roadmap to RICHE$ Personal Business Plan!**
  (8 Audio Tapes plus a Personal Study Guide)
- ❑ **The Safe Place Seminar**
  (4 Part Video Seminar plus a Dating Manual)
- ❑ **The Safe Place Workshop for Men . . . You CAN Change Your Lady!**
  (6 Audio Tapes plus Personal Study Guide)
- ❑ **The Safe Place Workshop for Women . . . You CAN Change Your Man!**
  (6 Audio Tapes plus Personal Study Guide)
- ❑ **Lifestyle Selling!**
  (4 Audio Tapes for Sales and Management)
- ❑ **Sexual Addiction and the Search for Intimacy**
  (7 Part Video Seminar)
- ❑ **Maximum Marriage**
  (4 Part Video Seminar)
- ❑ **AA: Anyone Anonymous**
  (6 Part Video Seminar plus Book)
- ❑ **WWJD? Game Plan for Living**
  (8 Audio Tapes plus Book)

To Order or to Receive a Catalog:

Website:	http//www.timtimmons.com
Fax:	(972) 248-4815
Phone:	(972) 248-4411
E-mail:	TIM@timtimmons.com
Write:	GPFL Enterprises
	4570 Westgrove, Suite 220
	Addison, TX 75248

To order additional copies of

Roadmap to Riche$

send $24.95 plus 4.95 shipping and handling to

Books, Etc.
PO Box 1406
Mukilteo, WA 98275

or have your credit card ready and call

(800) 917-BOOK